WHEN THE DANUBE RAN RED

Religion, Theology, and the Holocaust

WHEN
THE
DANUBE
RAN
RED

•

Zsuzsanna Ozsváth

With a foreword by David Patterson

Syracuse University Press

Publication of this book is made possible through the generous support
of both the Leah and Paul Lewis Chair in Holocaust Studies and the
School of Arts and Humanities at the University of Texas at Dallas.

For a listing of books published and distributed by Syracuse University Press,
visit our Web site at SyracuseUniversityPress.syr.edu.

ISBN: 978-0-8156-0980-3

Library of Congress Cataloging-in-Publication Data

Ozsváth, Zsuzsanna, 1934–
When the Danube ran red / Zsuzsanna Ozsváth ; with a foreword by David Patterson. — 1st ed.
p. cm. — (Religion, theology, and the Holocaust)
ISBN 978-0-8156-0980-3 (cloth : alk. paper)
1. Ozsváth, Zsuzsanna, 1934– —Childhood and youth.   2. Holocaust, Jewish
(1939–1945)—Hungary—Personal narratives.   3. Jewish children in the Holocaust—
Hungary—Budapest—Biography.   4. Jews—Hungary—Budapest—Biography.   5. Jewish
ghettos—Hungary—Budapest—History—20th century.   6. Holocaust survivors—Biography.
7. Fajó, Erzsébet, d. 1995.   8. Righteous Gentiles in the Holocaust—Hungary—Budapest—
Biography.   9. Budapest (Hungary)—Biography.   I. Title.
DS135.H93O97 2010
940.53'18092—dc22
[B]   2010017944

Manufactured in the United States of America

In memory of Erzsébet Fajó, who saved our lives

Zsuzsanna Ozsváth holds the Leah and Paul Lewis Chair in Holocaust Studies and is Professor of Literature and the History of Ideas in the School of Arts and Humanities at the University of Texas at Dallas. Ozsváth's research comprises two areas: the literature of the Holocaust and poetry translation. She has cotranslated (with Fred Turner) *Foamy Sky: The Poetry of Miklós Radnóti* and *The Iron-Blue Vault: The Poetry of Attila József,* and she is the author of *In the Footsteps of Orpheus: The Life and Times of Miklós Radnóti,* in addition to a large number of articles, translations, and cotranslations in a wide variety of journals. Her newest essays are "Foreseeing Destruction in the Work of Miklós Radnóti"; "From Country to Country: My Search for Home" in *The Writer Uprooted: Contemporary Jewish Exile Literature;* and "Trauma and Distortion: Holocaust Fiction and the Ban on Jewish Memory" in *The Holocaust in Hungary: Sixty Years After.*

CONTENTS

Contents

ILLUSTRATIONS

FOREWORD

David Patterson

Zsuzsanna Ozsváth opens her extraordinary remembrance of the Holocaust horror with the memory of a child: a little girl named Hanna (like the mother of the prophet Samuel), a survivor who had fled to Hungary from a mass grave called Poland. Thus from the outset Ozsváth presents us with two designated targets in the Nazis' extermination of the Jews: memory and the child. Elie Wiesel and Primo Levi, independently of each other, have described the Holocaust as a war against memory.[1] And wherever there is a war against memory, there is a war against the child, against the one to whom all memory is transmitted and in whom all memory lives. "It was as though the Nazi killers knew precisely what children represent to us," says Wiesel. "According to our tradition, the entire world subsists thanks to them."[2] But it was not *as though:* the Nazis knew precisely what they were doing when they systematically murdered more than a million and a half Jewish children: they were destroying not only a people but a world, a memory and a name, what in Hebrew is called *yad vashem.*

---

1. See Elie Wiesel, *Evil and Exile,* trans. Jon Rothschild (Notre Dame: Univ. of Notre Dame Press, 1990), 155; Primo Levi, *The Drowned and the Saved,* trans. Raymond Rosenthal (New York: Vintage Books, 1989), 31.

2. Elie Wiesel, *A Jew Today,* trans. Marion Wiesel (New York: Random House, 1978), 178–79.

Contained in these pages is the memory of a childhood forever undone and of a world forever lost. And yet in these pages the trace of a childhood and a remnant of a world are recovered, thanks to the courage and the art of Zsuzsanna Ozsváth. Crucial to this recovery is the testimony and the memory of one of the righteous, a girl named Erzsi, who herself was hardly more than a child. She is among those honored along the Avenue of the Righteous at Yad Vashem, the Holocaust Memorial and Archive Center in Jerusalem: it was her act of righteousness that made this memory possible. Thanks to Erzsi, we have this memory of a Jewish child from a world in which the very presence of a Jewish child was deemed a crime against humanity. The Jewish child is Zsuzsanna Ozsváth; the world is the world of Hungarian Jewry.

The World of Hungarian Jewry: The Memoir's Context

In Ozsváth's memoir one discovers not only the tale of a Jewish child marked for murder but also the tale of a world marked for obliteration, the world of Hungarian Jewry. With all the acumen of the scholar that she is, Ozsváth has already deftly portrayed that world as it was on the eve of the Holocaust in her book *In the Footsteps of Orpheus: The Life and Times of Miklós Radnóti*. In that book, which might be viewed as a companion work to her memoir, we see how the life and the poetry of Radnóti embodied the life of Hungarian Jews and their frustrated attempts to fit into a world that would have nothing to do with them *as Jews*. Indeed, Radnóti's voice was, in a very important sense, the voice of Hungarian Jewry. What modernity has demonstrated to Hungarian Jewry is that a world that would have nothing to do with them is a world that in the end will exterminate them. How did the story of Hungarian Jewry become a story of extermination? Answering that question is a key to understanding the vast historical context of this very personal memoir.

Jews have lived in Hungary for at least a thousand years. When the Crusaders arrived in the region in 1097, King Coloman refused to cooperate with them in their efforts to murder the Jews as they had in the Rhineland. Subsequent centuries saw a sequence of events familiar to Jews throughout Europe: expulsions, readmissions, forced conversions, persecutions, and more expulsions came one after the other. On August 29, 1526, the Turks defeated the Hungarians at the Battle of Mohács and dispersed some Jews to Turkish lands, where they generally fared better than the Jews who remained under Christian rule. When the Habsburgs recaptured Buda on September 2, 1686, Hungarian Jewry once more came under an ironfisted affliction at the hands of the Christians. On March 15, 1783, the Jews saw some relief, when Joseph II, son of Empress Maria Theresa, revoked the oppressive measures his mother had forced upon the Jews. By the mid–nineteenth century more and more Jews were adopting the Magyar language, reforming their religion, and making other efforts to fit into Hungarian society in the hope of gaining the same rights as other Hungarian citizens. Not until December 22, 1867, however, under the rule of Emperor Franz Joseph, would the Hungarian Parliament enact laws granting equal rights to the Jews.

The First World War resulted in the dissolution of the Austro-Hungarian Empire. With the signing of the Treaty of Trianon on June 4, 1920, Hungary lost two-thirds of its territory. Within months Miklós Horthy's reactionary forces came into power; with Horthy came yet another brutal repression of Hungarian Jewry. From 1920 onward Horthy's governments passed a series of anti-Jewish policies that intensified in 1938 and continued into the war years. In March 1939 the Hungarian Labor Service System, drafting Jewish men between the ages of eighteen and forty-eight into forced labor units, was established. In November 1940 Hungary became an ally of Germany, and in July and August 1941 the Hungarian government deported 20,000 "foreign" Jews, mostly from Ruthenia to Kemenets-Podolsk, where they were murdered by SS killing units. As the war continued, the Labor Service System developed into a form of systematic murder. Approximately 42,000 labor-service Jews were murdered on the Soviet front from 1942 to 1943. With the tide clearly turning against them in 1944, the Nazis grew concerned that the

Hungarians might work out a separate peace with the Allies, and that the Germans might not be able to complete the Final Solution to the Jewish Question before the war's end. On March 18, 1944, Hitler summoned Regent Horthy to the Schloss Klessheim in Austria to inform him that the Hungarians would continue in their capacity as Germany's ally and that Operation Margarete, the occupation of Hungary and the extermination of Hungarian Jewry, would commence immediately. In charge of the Operation were Adolf Eichmann, Dieter Wisliceny, and Hermann A. Krumey.

The first transport of Hungarian Jews arrived in Auschwitz on May 2, 1944, with the massive deportations beginning on May 15. Hungary's fascist prime minister Döme Sztójay and his henchmen László Endre and László Baky proved to be avid assistants to Eichmann in the program of extermination. By July 8 more than 437,000 Hungarian Jews had been sent to Auschwitz; 90 percent went directly from the trains to the gas chambers. Most of the Hungarian Jews who perished in the murder camp came from the Hungarian countryside; in Budapest, 100,000 Jews survived. Almost all of them, however, including Ozsváth and her family, endured the horrible conditions of the Budapest Ghetto. On October 15 Hungarian Nazi Ferenc Szálasi and the Arrow Cross Party led a coup to overthrow Horthy, who had been less than an enthusiastic partner with the Nazis. The Arrow Cross undertook a campaign of murdering Jews and shot thousands of Jews along the banks of the Danube—a crime that Zsuzsanna witnessed with her own child's eyes, when the Danube ran red with blood. On January 18, 1945, Soviet troops captured Budapest, and for the Jews of Hungary the war came to an end—but not before 550,000 of them had been murdered.

The Essence of the Holocaust

The Danube River that ran red with Jewish blood flowed into the sea, where the blood of the Jews was added to the oceans of the planet. The earth is awash in Jewish blood—literally. Just as it is covered with Jewish ashes—literally. In the time of the Holocaust, the smoke from burning Jewish bodies bellowed into the air for a thousand days from dozens of chimneys. The winds have cast the ashes of those millions of Jewish fathers, mothers, and children over the face of the earth. From that earth we now harvest our bread, and in our bread abide the ashes of the Jewish dead. They are woven into the fabric of humanity, body and soul: the essence of the Holocaust is part of our own essence. How could the extermination of a people have taken place in the heart of Christendom, at the hands of the most highly educated, most "enlightened" people on the planet? As we ponder this question, we come to a devastating realization: the Holocaust happened *precisely because* the Jews were trapped in the heart of European Christendom, where they fell prey to a certain strain of the thinking born of the Enlightenment.

With the spread of Christianity in the early centuries of the common era, Jew hatred assumed theological dimensions. Saint Ambrose, bishop of Milan, called for the burning of synagogues. Saint John Chrysostom labeled the Jews as enemies of God and was among the first to level against them the charge of deicide. And Saint Augustine viewed the exile of the Jews in the Diaspora as a divine punishment for rejecting Christianity. The first mass murders of the Jews at the hands of the Christians came with the launching of the First Crusade in 1096, when tens of thousands of Jews were slaughtered in the Rhineland. The first recorded Blood Libel, the claim that Jews used the blood of Christian children to make their Passover matzo, came from Saint William of Norwich in 1144. By the end of the thirteenth century Jews were said to be agents of Satan, desecrators of the Host, sorcerers, and vampires. Over the subsequent centuries the Jews were expelled at one time or another *from every country* in Europe.

With the dawn of the Enlightenment in the eighteenth century, what had been a theological hatred of the Jews became a philosophical hatred. Almost every intellectual giant of modernity, from Voltaire to Kant, from Hegel to Schopenhauer, issued diatribes against the Jews. And the ideologues of National Socialism were the heirs to that tradition. At the opening of the June 1939 meeting of the National Socialist Association of University Lecturers, Professor Walter Schultze declared, "What the great thinkers of German Idealism dreamed of . . . finally comes alive, assumes reality."[3] With the advent of Nazi Germany, the Kantian position that a human being is "determinable only by laws which he gives to himself,"[4] which prefigures the Heideggerian assertion that the "will to power designates the basic character of beings,"[5] became a defining feature of the National Socialist reality, a reality that allowed no place for Jews. For the very presence of Jews in the world signifies a teaching and a tradition that are anathema to this defining feature of Nazi ideology. Therefore the annihilation of European Jewry is not merely a case of racism run amok. It had little to do with scapegoating, economic envy, xenophobia, or the Treaty of Versailles. The Nazis were not anti-Semites because they were racists; rather, they were racists because they were anti-Semites. An anti-Semitic foundation of the ideology had to be determined in order to arrive at the racist position.

Central to any ideology is a basic view of what imparts value to the human being. According to the Nazis, the value of a human being is determined first of all by an accident of nature: one who is born an "Aryan" already has more value than one who is not. And if you are an Aryan, you can take on even greater substance through the will to power. According to the Jewish teaching that the Nazis set out to obliterate, a human being has value not because of anything that can be weighed or counted, measured or observed, but for having been created in the image and likeness of the Holy One. Judaism also teaches that all of humanity originated from a single human being, so that each of us

---

3. Quoted in George L. Mosse, *Nazi Culture* (New York: Grosset and Dunlop, 1966), 316.

4. Immanuel Kant, *The Critique of Practical Reason*, trans. Lewis White Beck (New York: Macmillan, 1985), 101.

5. Martin Heidegger, *Nietzsche*, vol. 1, trans. David Krell (San Francisco: Harper and Row, 1979), 18.

is connected to the other, both spiritually and physically, a connection that is most fundamentally expressed in an absolute responsibility of each for the other. Nothing could be more threatening to Nazi ideology. The Nazis' calculated, systematic assault on the divine spark within the human is a defining part of the singularity of the Holocaust.

That assault was carried out not just by murdering the body of Israel but by destroying souls before they destroyed bodies. The Nazis used the Jewish holy calendar to plan their actions against the Jews. Torah scrolls and synagogues were reduced to ashes. Cemeteries were destroyed or desecrated. By degrees the Nazis forbade mezuzahs and *mikvehs*, weddings and funerals, Sabbath observance and Torah study, all forms of prayer or piety. Pregnancy itself became a capital crime: if the sin of the Jew was being alive, there was no criminal more heinous than a Jewish mother. Slated for annihilation, then, were not only mothers and fathers and children, but the very notion of a mother, father, or child. Especially the child. With the Nazis' burning of the bodies of the little ones, it was as though creation itself had gone up in flames. All of creation, says the Talmud, is sustained by the breath of little children (*Shabbat* 119b). It is their lips that carry our prayers to God's ear, for their lips are untainted by sin.[6] When they robbed the Jewish people of their children, it was as if the Nazis had rendered God deaf to the cries of the Jews. It was as if God were dead.

Because Zsuzsanna's story is a child's story, this defining aspect of the Holocaust is worth a moment's reflection. The most overwhelming of the memorials at Yad Vashem is the Children's Memorial. Entering the memorial is like entering a tomb. But there are no bodies laid to rest in the tomb. On the contrary, there is an abysmal sense of unrest. That is the reason for the handrails: it is not the darkness—it is the swoon that comes over you as the ground crumbles from beneath your feet. The

---

6. See Eliyahu Kitov, *The Book of Our Heritage*, vol. 1, trans. Nathan Bluman (New York: Feldheim Publishers, 1973), 75–76.

inner space of the memorial is filled with a darkness seared by a million and a half points of light generated by mirrors reflecting the light of five candles. Every few seconds you hear the name, the age, and the birthplace of a murdered child. Every few seconds your soul is wracked not by the million and a half little ones but by *this one*. The researchers at Yad Vashem have identified fewer than a third of the names of the murdered children. It takes three years to get through the list.

The children were among those who were first targeted for extermination, not only to annihilate the Jewish future but also to destroy the Jewish tradition. Many texts from the tradition attest to the importance of the child, both to the life of the teaching and to the Holy One whose presence is revealed through the tradition. In the Midrash it is written, "Come and see how beloved are the children by the Holy One, blessed be He. The Sanhedrin [official Jewish councils] were exiled but the Shekhinah [Divine Presence] did not go into exile with them. When, however, the children were exiled, the Shekhinah went into exile with them" (*Eichah Rabbah* 1:6:33). And in the *Tikunei Zohar,* it is taught that children are "the face of the Shekhinah."[7] Because children are the face of the Divine Presence, the Nazis eradicated that presence by creating realms that were void of Jewish children. I have read Holocaust memoirs in which survivors relate that they did not see a child for as long as five years, and more. In the anti-world engineered by the Nazis—a realm whose essence is not just murder but the murder of *children*—those who are nearest to God are precisely the ones most distant from God's help. That is why the child is the one nearest to our memory, the one who invades our memory, inexorably, as in this memoir by Zsuzsanna Ozsváth.

But there is more, something central to the significance of the memory and the name that define Ozsváth's memoir and the testimony

7. Cited in Nehemia Polen, *The Holy Fire: The Teachings of Rabbi Kalonymus Kalman Shapira* (Northvale, NJ: Jason Aronson, 1999), 102.

it transmits. In the attempt to annihilate the souls of the Jews, the Nazis obliterated their names. In order to receive their meager rations in the camps, for instance, Jews had to identify themselves by the numbers tattooed into their flesh. If the name is the vessel of the soul, the face is its manifestation. And so the Holocaust is in its essence a radical assault on the face. The great sage of the Talmud, Rabbi Akiba, maintains that the humanity and the dignity of the human being are revealed in the face; in the face lies the image and likeness of the Holy One,[8] which is most fundamentally manifest in the prohibition against murder. The Nazi *must* obliterate the face of the Jew, for the Nazi's aim is to eliminate the *absolute* nature of the prohibition against murder. Of course, the face not only forbids us to murder—it commands us to offer a kind word and a helping hand. In every such action there abides a mystery, the mystery of the holy that abides in the face. Zsuzsanna's story is the story of how that holiness, that divine spark, came under assault. It is also the story of the miracle and the mystery of one who helped, one of the Righteous, whose name was Erzsi and who had the face of an angel.

The Uniqueness of This Memory of a Unique Horror

Several thousand survivors have written their memoirs of the Holocaust. This one, however, has certain features that set it apart from the others. It is written not only in remembrance of the suffering inflicted upon the Jewish people at the hands of the Nazis and, in this case, at the hands of the Hungarians, but it is also a tribute to the righteousness of an individual who came to the rescue of a family. In moving portraits of the people in her childhood, one by one, Ozsváth demonstrates the scope of the Nazis' destruction, the destruction of people with names and faces, the annihilation of a culture, of a world. Hers is an account

---

8. See Louis Finkelstein, *Akiba: Scholar, Saint and Martyr* (New York: Atheneum, 1981), 103.

of the Nazi assault on a child, one that reveals the heinous nature of an evil that draws children into its net of death. The child called Zsuzsi, however, grew up to become the renowned Holocaust scholar Dr. Zsuzsanna Ozsváth. Therefore her tale is written from the deeply informed viewpoint of a scholar, as well as from the impassioned viewpoint of a survivor. She has a profound understanding of what the annihilation of the Jewish people meant specifically to Hungarian Jews: interwoven with her testimony is a revealing account—a much-needed account—of Hungarian history. Thus she offers not only the singular tale of her own family but also a singular view of what lay behind the Holocaust itself.

As an award-winning translator of Hungarian poetry, moreover, the author of this work possesses an artistic talent that is rare in any writer. Every page is written in a beautiful, moving, engaging style that brings out not only the evil confronted but also the holiness of the life that survives the confrontation; unlike most memoirs, this one is truly a work of *literature*. Thus Ozsváth weaves a tale, as well as tales within the tale, with a literary skill and an insight that make this one difficult to put down: it is riveting.

From the moment we meet Hanna and the testimony from one child to another on the Nazi horror, we are haunted by an ominous foreboding. That foreboding becomes the motif of the little girl's desperate concern for her father: the one source of assurance, of humanity and truth, in her child's world, the one whose eyes and whose words conveyed to her a glimpse of what she feared most. Well before the Nazis began the Hungarian deportations in 1944, Zsuzsanna and her family were enduring an assault on their souls, a point that becomes increasingly clear with every page we read. As she relates the cataclysm of Hungarian history between the lines of her childhood memory, we see her childlike innocence in failing to understand that the Nazis want to kill them merely because they are Jews. In her child's question a most profound question concerning the very meaning of our humanity devolves upon us.

I have suggested that another central figure in this tale had the face of an angel. Anyone who has seen her photo from that time, as I have, would surely agree. It is not for nothing that, with her persistent literary art, Ozsváth introduces us to Erzsi with her dream of angels whose faces are Erzsi's face. This initial portrayal of Erzsi is brilliantly set against the background of the deadly Hungarian labor details, the waves of suicides, and the Germans' entry into Budapest, all amidst Zsuzsanna's attempts to maintain some semblance of a normal childhood. By the time she was eight years old, however, her childhood was anything but "normal." The mounting presence of the murderers in their midst led Zsuzsanna's family to ponder the impossible decision forced upon so many Jewish families: should they leave or should they stay? Reading Zsuzsanna's account, we find an answer to a common question, a question that rests upon a common misunderstanding of the Holocaust: "Why didn't the Jews leave?" Their options were few to nonexistent. At that moment, when nothing but the abyss lay before Zsuzsi's family, Erzsi stepped forward when the world had turned away.

As Zsuzsanna relates the story of being forced into the Budapest Ghetto, we begin to perceive the pattern of history—both personal and world historical—that unfolds in this beautifully conceived work: first life is normal, then legal measures are passed to remove the Jews from human society. Next they must leave their homes, their property is confiscated, and the Jews themselves are isolated, in preparation for being annihilated. The chilling realization hits us: in Nazi Europe every Jew was rendered *homeless* before being murdered. And yet we see Zsuzsanna's determined persistence in maintaining a semblance of life when surrounded by death: in her play, in her studies, and in her piano practice. Indeed, we see this child clinging to the literary and artistic icons of Western civilization, even as that civilization was collapsing all around her. Here, too, we encounter the personal deftly interwoven with the world historical. For with a terrible and terrifying irony that conveys beneath its surface the meaning of the Holocaust for civilization, Zsuzsanna persisted in practicing the civilization's music. This dedication unfolds on the eve of the realization of Zsuzsanna's worst fears: the separation from her family.

Her simple yet compelling narration of this fear brings out the Nazi assault on the soul—on the soul of a child—that goes to the core of the Holocaust. Chapter 24, "Alone," is one of the most chilling in this remarkable book. Here the child is turned over to the horror that has been stalking her: utter separation from her family, ferociously alone and abandoned, as the city is being reduced to rubble and the people who remain alive are reduced to little more than animals, scavenging for any food they can find. In the bombardment this child endured and the ravaging hunger she suffered we see what the Nazis inflicted upon the body of Israel. In the sight of Jews murdered and shoved into the Danube—the blue river that now ran red—we see, through her child's eyes, what the Nazis inflicted upon the souls of the Jews.

Thus a little girl called Zsuzsi—who would become a concert pianist, the translator of Hungary's most famous Holocaust poet Miklós Radnóti, and an internationally established Holocaust scholar—survived the Nazi assault on the Jews in a city that lost more than 160,000 people. She had seen the face of profound evil, yes. But she had also beheld the face of miraculous goodness, the face of an angel named Erzsi. Conveying that vision, this memoir restores the face that the Nazis set out to erase: the face of a child that puts to us the question put to the first human being: Where are you? The tale before us, therefore, is not a "feel-good" piece. It has no "happy ending." Indeed, it has no ending at all. No sooner are we reassured by the life-saving righteousness of Erzsi than we are implicated by it. Like all of the righteous, her example robs us of our excuses. And in the wake of the question put to the first human being come the questions put to his firstborn, Cain: "Where is your brother?" And: "What have you done?"

August 2009

ACKNOWLEDGMENTS

The large story of my life that played itself out during the Holocaust comprises many small, individual stories about which I have often spoken to my family, friends, and students. They are part of my life, my past, and my present. But as time has gone by, I have suddenly and unexpectedly felt a great need to tell the whole, larger story, starting with the time when I first heard about the atrocities the Germans committed against the Jews, continuing with Erzsi, the young girl who risked her life over and over again while saving ours, and ending the tale with our long walk home in the streets of burned-out Budapest. Writing down this tale went very fast. Living under its spell for a lifetime, I felt relieved to be speaking about it in a book. After a while, I also knew it had to be done. For one quiet morning in Budapest, many years ago, my mother spoke to me about our obligation to recall the past, "lest thou forget the things which thine eyes saw, and lest they depart from thy heart all the days of thy life; but make them known unto thy children and thy children's children" (Deuteronomy 4:9). So I have written this book.

I acknowledge my gratitude to Mimi and Mitch Barnett, who created the Leah and Paul Lewis Chair at the University of Texas at Dallas, which made it possible for me to work on research projects during the summers; in addition, I am grateful for the care and attention they give this program. Also, I am deeply indebted for the sustained help of Provost Hobson Wildenthal, whose interest in the Holocaust and belief in the importance of studying it have been instrumental in teaching and building the program around this event in the School of Arts and Humanities at U.T. Dallas.

Also, I wish to thank Paul Cornelius, who has given me his invaluable assistance in the process of improving and tightening earlier versions of this manuscript; and I would like to express my deepest gratitude to Mei Lin Turner, who has not only offered me generous editorial advice but also prepared this text for publication.

In addition, I have greatly benefited from the encouragement and help of Professor Michael Simpson and Mr. George Core, editor of *The Sewanee Review,* as both emphasized and expressed again and again their dedication to, and support of, my work.

And I am deeply grateful to my friends and family as well, especially to our son-in-law, Gary Bernardini, who encouraged me to write this book, and to our son, Peter, without whose unstinting help and encouragement these pages would not have seen the light of day. I would also like to tell our daughter, Kathleen; daughter-in-law, Shevi; and two grandchildren, Elizabeth and Eliana, that they are our source of love and happiness in the world.

My greatest debt, however, is to my husband, István, who stood by me during the hardest times of my life. He is my companion, my love, my friend, my advisor, and my critic. Without him, I could not have recovered from the wounds of the Holocaust, overcome the tragic death of my parents, raised my wonderful family, or written this book.

WHEN THE DANUBE RAN RED

1

HANNA

It was evening, I remember, and I was in the third grade. Darkness settled outside, and only the streetlights lit up my room. The long, strange shadows of tree branches stretched along the wall. I cowered on my favorite pillow, whose embroidery showed a happy dachshund in a red-blue-green orchard. I held my dolls in my arms and waited for my father. My stomach trembled, my hands shook: I could not forget what Hanna had told me earlier in the afternoon.

It began when we were standing in line for a slice of the chocolate birthday cake, adorned with shiny pearly hearts and red candles, at the party of my best friend, Márta. It was then that Hanna started to speak to me about the Germans. Hanna was not in my class; I met her in the house of my parents' friends. But I knew that she had arrived here with her mother after escaping from Poland. She spoke Hungarian fluently; she also told stories about the Germans that made me shiver. Of course, Hanna was not the only one who spoke about the Germans and their assaults on the Jews; some of my parents' closest friends did the same. Yet what Hanna told me that day tore into me more deeply than any of the stories I had heard before.

The afternoon started out with me standing in line, playing with the children waiting for their slice of cake, including Juti (another close friend of mine), Márta, and Hanna. But after a while, I lost track of the others, listening only to what Hanna whispered into my ears. She spoke quickly, almost breathlessly, and soon I could pay attention to nothing but her story.

First, she told me about the morning of her seventh birthday, a year before, in a Polish town, the name of which I have now forgotten, where she had lived with her parents. Her mother woke her up early that day, Hanna said, telling her to hurry because soon they would have to leave their apartment. Receiving an order sent to every Jewish family in town the day before, Hanna's parents were warned to stay put in their dwelling and wait for further instructions. Everybody knew what this statement meant: the Jews would be driven out of their apartments. Hanna told me that her mother stayed up all night, packing their belongings in boxes, preparing a backpack for each of them for the journey. Then, in the small hours of the morning, she made chocolate milk, mixing *real* cocoa, sugar, and milk, all of which she bought from a peasant in exchange for her wedding ring. But Hanna had barely tasted her drink, the aroma of which, she told me crying, she still remembered, when their door was kicked in by the Germans, arriving with sticks and rifles, driving them from their apartment to the marketplace, as they did during that morning with the rest of the town's Jews. It was then in the marketplace that they separated the children from their parents, the old from the young.

At this moment, my heart tightened. I knew what would come. I had heard about such scenes before, and I feared them so much that at night, when I closed my eyes, I saw myself alone amid masses of people, some of them shot, some of them fleeing, with my parents lost in the helter-skelter. I was right: Hanna had described to me such a scene. After a while, the German soldiers marched her father and grandfather, together with a large group of men, into the nearby synagogue. Forcing them to stand for hours, the Germans tore up the place, throwing the Torah, the prayer books, and prayer shawls out of the windows onto the mud and dirt of the street, ordering the prisoners to pick up "the garbage." Then they drove the group back to the marketplace, where all the books and shawls were set ablaze. And while all of this was going on, the rest of the Jews in the marketplace, among them Hanna and her mother, had to stand and wait for hours without food and water. In the meantime, the Germans cut off the men's beards and earlocks, ordering some of them to dance, others to crawl on the ground, soon covered by mud and blood and ashes, before they shot them. The shooting went on all night. Among those killed were Hanna's father and grandfather, both of whom, Hanna swore, she recognized in the moonlight among the corpses, when she was moved after a while some rows down. They were lying in pools of blood. After executing all the men on the square, the Germans marched the women and children behind a wall, where the streets of the ghetto curved across.

At this point, I noticed that some of the adults around us, too, were intently listening to the story Hanna was recounting.

"What does the word *ghetto* mean?" I asked, terrified. The adults turned away.

Hanna rolled her eyes: "A place where Jews must live."

"And what if they don't want to live there?" I inquired.

"They will be shot."

I shuddered: What would happen to us? We don't live in a ghetto! Shouldn't we move into one? Are there ghettos in Hungary? Will the Germans build some for us?

After the massacre at the marketplace, Hanna told me, she stayed in the ghetto of the town with her mother and some of her relatives. Despite the fact that all their means of communication were cut off, the news of the killings in the marketplace reached her two cousins, who had lived in Warsaw under assumed names ever since the first day of the German occupation. And, as my father heard it later from an aunt of Hanna's, the young men decided to save the girl and her mother. In fact, the younger of the two, Andrzej, came to town to smuggle them out of the ghetto. At first, Hanna's mother did not want to leave, claiming that she believed her husband was hiding somewhere.

"He could have survived the shooting," she cried. "That Hanna saw him among the corpses doesn't mean he was shot dead. He might have only acted as if he were dead. In fact, he might still be alive, hiding somewhere and planning to return to us at the end of the war."

But Andrzej argued that if so, the family would be reunited after the war. Until then, he insisted, Hanna and her mother could best hide in Hungary, where the mother had grown up and where her parents still lived. This was true. Hanna's mother was, as my father told me later, homesick for Hungary throughout her years in Poland; now, her husband murdered, she became lonely, poor, and desolate. Small wonder that she gave in. In fact, after a while, as she told my mother, she started to look forward to the support she and Hanna would get from her parents. Escaping from the ghetto, they were smuggled out of Poland, driven across two countries, brought ultimately to Békéscsaba, a town in Hungary near the Romanian border, where Hanna's grandparents lived and also our family. Still, although their lives seemed to be quite secure right now, with tears in her eyes Hanna whispered to me that she was homeless here and that she was missing her father. In fact, she said, her voice breaking, she did not want to go on living without him.

Listening to Hanna, I did not look into her eyes while she spoke. I could not bear to look at her, thinking to myself all the time, "Perhaps she is lying?" I hoped she was.

Later, when I ran home from the birthday party through the dark streets of Békéscsaba, the wind and black rain against my face, my heart raced so fast that I could hardly breathe. I felt I was running for my life. When I arrived, I looked for my father in the pharmacy, located on the ground floor of the apartment building in which we lived. There he stood, tall and sweet, gleaming dark beautiful eyes, in a white coat as always. He was smiling, lifting me up high in his arms.

I trembled and sobbed, rubbing my face against his, telling him about Hanna, with fear and despair shaking me: "I don't want to march to the marketplace," I cried, holding him tight. "I don't want to be homeless; and I want to die rather than let you be taken away!"

"You don't have to be homeless," he said, "you won't have to die, and I won't be taken away." His loving-sweet smile lit up his face. He stroked my hair and added, "Go home! I'll be there in an hour or so."

4

I went up the stairs. By the time I had supper with my mother and Erzsi, our playmate and nanny, I felt a bit better, even calmer. But I was not interested in fairy tales nor in their discussions right now; neither did I wish to tell them what had happened to Hanna in the marketplace in Poland. I knew they would say, "She was lying."

I wanted to stay alone and wait for my father, with whom I could always speak about everything important. I trusted him infinitely, and I loved him endlessly. But now, as I sat by myself under the window, on my favorite pillow with the happy dachshund in the red-blue-green orchard, waiting for him, I could not forget what I had heard. All I saw before my eyes was Hanna's marketplace, covered with corpses. And by then, I knew what these corpses looked like: they were covered with blood, and some had their eyes open. Small wonder. I had heard them described again and again by people my parents knew, by people who had seen such corpses lying all over the place, by people who had come from some other country to Hungary, who apparently could talk of nothing but bloody corpses.

Sitting on the pillow, waiting for my father, I suddenly started to think of unbearably difficult questions: Would my father believe what I told him? Would he really talk with me about, and admit to, the danger threatening us? Or would he just want to calm me down as he always did? And then I thought of an even harder question: *Can* he really answer my questions? *Can* he foretell the future? For the first time in my life, I was unsure.

It was no coincidence, of course, that I was thinking of these questions. Hanna's story, however frightening, was not the first one of its kind I had encountered. As a matter of fact, this story took me back in time, reminding me of an experience I would not forget for as long as I lived. This experience was older than the horror stories people were talking about regarding the Germans and the Jews in Poland, older than the shootings in Hanna's marketplace. It was, in fact, the experience that had started all my nightmares. And seeing now the marketplace before my eyes, I remembered this experience, the threat of which had made my blood run cold for a long time.

Sitting and waiting for my father, I recalled that other day, which had begun, I will never forget, quietly, almost happily. It developed, however, into one of terrible fright and confusion during the afternoon. We had just finished lunch. My mother was in the kitchen; Erzsi and I were playing our version of Winnie the Pooh: I was the Queen of England, Erzsi was Kanga. We sat around the dining-room table, talking to one another in low voices. Suddenly, pale and disturbed, my father appeared in the doorway.

I knew that something had happened and immediately asked him, "What is wrong"?

"Nothing," he said, with a desperate grin on his face, "just go on playing."

I did not believe him, but I did not know what to say. He came inside, sat down, and turned on the radio. This, too, was strange. He usually had no time to leave the pharmacy, and he certainly had never turned on the radio during the day. But now he did, and he seemed agitated. Listening to the news (which I heard as well, but did not quite understand), he stretched out his arms, and uttered a sentence that made me terribly worried, a sentence I have never forgotten, one that makes me tremble even today:

"Everything is over."

I noticed that his face was distorted, and I saw tremendous fear and confusion in his eyes. In fact, I saw that he was frightened to death. Later, and over the years again and again, I overheard my mother telling friends that on this afternoon, on March 12, 1938, when my father came upstairs from the pharmacy to listen to the radio announce the *Anschluss* (the German occupation of Austria and the country's annexation to the Reich), he immediately understood and foresaw the consequences of this event. I threw myself into his lap, clutching his neck. For the first time in my life, I saw his face changing, fear clouding his eyes. Later, I recognized the same fear in other people's eyes as well, whenever they discussed politics, listened to the news, or whispered to one another horrific stories about the atrocities the Germans were committing against the Jews. And I have never forgotten his words: "Everything is over." In fact, the more years passed by, the more I understood that by March 1938, he recognized the nature and meaning as well as the life-threatening reality of the Nazis' hatred of the Jews.

Over the years, again and again, I wanted to talk about this with him, but I could not. As soon as I started to speak or ask him about his remark that "everything" was "over," he began to discuss something else. Throwing me into the air, begging me to play the piano, talking about music, discussing poems, fairy tales, or butterflies with me, he obviously wanted to divert my attention from the Germans' attacks against the Jews. But each time we heard about them, I could see that he was frightened and overwhelmed by the news. And while I noticed his despair, he tried to act as if things would work out just fine. In fact, he tried to remain calm in front of us, even after the Germans' march into Czechoslovakia, about which I had heard from children who had fled from Prague to Poland, and then again, from Poland to Hungary. And he showed great strength when I asked him questions, talking to me about what had happened, assuring me again and again that if a world war came about, it would soon end, because the Germans would lose, the Allies would win, and, in the end, America would protect the Jews of Europe. That is, we would survive. But I could not help my fear. I remembered his despair and heard his words when Germany annexed Austria.

"So what is true? Is he or isn't he still thinking that *everything* is *over?*" I asked myself again and again over the years; and I feared that he still thought it was.

Then, one day, I learned from Erzsi that he had tried to secure visas, attempting to move me and Iván to Switzerland. And that after the Swiss Embassy had refused to consider our application, he and my mother had started to study Portuguese, because they believed we would be able to emigrate to Brazil. While I had noticed that my parents were studying

Portuguese, I did not know that they wanted to leave Hungary. Why? And to emigrate to Brazil? Why? When I asked him directly, he told me that life had become very difficult for Jews in Europe and that to live in Brazil would be much better for us. But when I asked him what would happen if we did not succeed in going away, he started to speak about other things. Again I knew that he was not telling me the truth.

Now that I was waiting for him under the window, on the night of Márta's birthday party, I hoped I could straighten things out. I wanted him to talk with me about everything. I decided to ask him directly: How would we be able to avoid the marketplace, where Hanna's father had been murdered in Poland? My body was trembling.

Then he arrived, and light filled up the room. Tall and strong and lovely to the eye, he took me in his arms.

"Are you still thinking about the birthday party this afternoon, darling?" he asked. "Don't you worry. Remember what I told you! We are together now and will be together forever. What the Germans did in Poland could never happen in Hungary! Never! Hungarians wouldn't allow it!"

He was right, I thought, obviously they would not. Looking at him, I felt stronger, better, less frightened. He was so confident and so handsome, and I loved him so much.

When he left, I fell asleep; but I had bad dreams. I heard shooting from the street and saw Germans pulling the beards of men and cutting the hair of women. I took a lock of my own dark hair in my hand and cried at the thought of losing it. Then I saw my father shot, lying in a pool of blood, and myself, running across the street. Alone.

Later that evening, my brother came home with his friends. I opened my eyes and saw them; but soon I fell asleep. When the boys left, Iván woke me up. I admired his beautifully carved, intelligent face, blond hair, light-brown eyes. I wished to know: Was he afraid as well? But all he wanted was to talk with me about a red car he had seen that day and would like to drive when he grew up. I did not want to listen; nor would I tell him why I was crying. He went to the kitchen, stuffed his pockets full of lemon candy, and returned. But I did not want any. He tried to tell me more about the red car, but I did not want to hear it: I was terribly afraid. Then he got bored with me. He started to recite our nightly farewell ritual.

"Dream of fairies and angels." I replied, as ever.

"You, of the wide blue sky."

"And you of even more beautiful things."

"OK."

"Then, let's sleep."

It took a while before I fell asleep, though. And as soon as I did, I found myself back at the marketplace, the site of my first dream that night. But this time, I saw my mother, father, Iván, Erzsi, as well as myself, dead—shot by the Germans. Lying in blood, at least we were all together.

2

RELOCATIONS

The impact of Hanna's story on my life was immediate and overwhelming. Recalling those times, I remember waking up night upon night, screaming, "They shot my father! They shot my father! Let's run!" Or I cried in despair, "We are homeless! We are homeless!"

My parents tried their best to reassure me, telling me again and again that there was no danger threatening us. At one point, I decided to avoid political discussions with children and grown-ups alike. Before Márta's birthday party, I had been eager to listen to the exchanges my parents had with their friends regarding Hitler, the Third Reich, and the lot of the Jews in Austria and Poland. In fact, I had sat through these discussions, paying attention to the opinions of everybody. Horror-stricken and trembling, I still wanted to know "what had happened." After Hanna's account of the shootings, however, I ran from the room when my parents listened to the radio and fled when I heard people discussing the news or the consequences of the recent restrictions imposed on Jews in Hungary. Of course, I was not alone in my desire to hide from these tales; my parents also found it reassuring that I did so. Worried about the trauma Hanna's account had brought to my life, they wanted me to avoid, and encouraged others to stop, all discussions of this sort in the future. In this way, they hoped I would be able to sleep again, forget about the danger, and suppress, perhaps even overcome, the shock Hanna's devastating story had created in me.

As my mother later admitted, she asked all of our friends and relatives to stop describing their own experiences of the atrocities the Germans committed in occupied Europe, as well as discussing the latest news about the fate of the Jews that was circulating in the city. While the whispering among people never died away, for the moment I ceased to listen to it. In fact, I did not want to hear these stories; nor did I wish to think about them. To accomplish my goal, I avoided meeting Hanna in the street as well as in school. Slowly, descending to the deepest layers of my memory, her tale, I believe, faded away after a while, turning into a bad dream, parts of nightmares, and various inexplicable feelings, fears, or shapeless recollections. As a result, at least on the surface, I stopped thinking about the marketplace, where the murdered Jews lay on top of one another in heaps, as Hanna had described them to me. In fact, I almost forgot about the mass shootings in the Polish marketplace. Almost.

But then, much later, I think, in the summer of 1941, I overheard some agitated, bitter discussions between my parents and relatives regarding the third set of anti-Jewish laws in Hungary. At this point, nobody withdrew to another room to discuss the danger, nor could I run away from the news. My parents, their siblings, friends, and acquaintances complained and argued with one another about the new laws that would be legislated against us and the impossibility of escaping these horrors— with nobody caring too much about the presence or absence of Iván and me in the room. Listening to these discussions, both of us noticed that despite the threat everybody saw arising, there was a remarkable contrast between the conclusions people drew: between their bleak view regarding the future and the strangely optimistic remarks with which their discussions on the anti-Jewish laws always ended.

As my aunt Anni, said, "On the other hand, . . . no matter how humiliating and threatening these laws appear to be, we must remember that they will legislate nothing *worse* than what we already have. And in this context, we must realize that our lives are not threatened by them."

Or as Uncle Imre said, "True. It is horrible, horrible. But whatever is taking place, we are still alive. Therefore," he said with great emphasis and relief, "however miserable we feel at times, we must regard ourselves as especially and extraordinarily lucky."

And I overheard my grandfather's remark: "Although Horthy [the regent] has to make concessions to Hitler, in the end, he won't let the worst happen: he will save the Jews of Hungary."

There was no doubt in my mind that these observations were true. I learned only much later, as an adult, and only after I had left Hungary, that these were not reliable observations, but rather unreal assumptions, driven by hope, explicable only by the mentality of people who knew they were sentenced to death, people who, understandably, could not live with this knowledge. Under the unbearable pressure, they tried to act as if nothing were wrong, thereby suppressing the inevitability of their sentence. For Horthy did very little to save the Jews in Hungary. Although, finally, in the summer of 1944, under tremendous pressure and threat, he stopped the deportation of the Jews of Budapest to Auschwitz, he did nothing for the 20,000 "foreign Jews" captured, deported, and shot into mass graves at Kemenets-Podolsk in August 1941; nor did he even attempt to stop the draft, torture, and murder of 42,000 Jewish men in labor service on the front during the years 1941 to 1943; or the ghettoization and deportation of 437,000 Jews—men, women, children, the sick, and the aged—by the Hungarian gendarmerie, who locked their victims into boxcars directed to Auschwitz in the late spring and early summer of 1944. Of course, one cannot foresee the future. Yet it's worthwhile to note the gap between my family's hopes for survival and the reality of the Jews' murder. In 1941, when I heard again and again about the "regent's benevolence" toward the Jews, I, like most people in my family, believed the story. In fact, seeing Horthy's stately figure, silver hair, grandfatherly smile, and "kind looks" in the newspapers and newsreels again and again, I did not doubt that he wanted to help us survive.

Interestingly enough, however, I noticed that my father did not join the choir that sang the praises of the regent. I understood this in the first place because after a while, he started to talk to me about politics as if I were an adult. Answering my questions, he was eager to point to Horthy's complicity in the mass killings of Jews during the counterrevolution in 1919, a phase during which several of his friends had been killed, and in the "Jew-beatings" at the universities in the early 1920s, of which my father himself had been a victim. In addition, he emphasized Horthy's willingness to support anti-Semitic legislation at the end of the 1930s and beginning of the 1940s. Still, as he explained, he hoped for Horthy's defense of the Jews, not because he thought that the regent liked them, but because he believed that Horthy was aware of both the impending defeat of the Reich and his own responsibility for the lives of hundreds of thousands of human beings. Hence, at the end of the day, my father said, he thought that Horthy would refuse Hitler's plan to expel and murder all the Jews of Hungary. My father was right. But only partly so. We learned the facts much later. On the one hand, Horthy wanted the Germans' help to negotiate the return of the country's territories, which had been taken from Hungary after World War I by the harsh Peace Treaty of Trianon (1920). Using his plans for their own purposes, the parties of the Hungarian ultra-Right celebrated National Socialism, formulating harsh anti-Jewish laws, which crippled the Jewish community. In this way, Hungary paid back the Reich for its help in reversing the unjust treaty. The country even showed itself willing to rearm and mobilize, supporting thereby the German plan for establishing the "New Order" in Europe. On the other hand, Horthy obviously knew that Hitler would lose the war, and then Hungary would be looked upon as a partner of the Reich in the mass murder of the Jews. Hence, he tried to avoid their deportation from Hungary.

But when the Germans occupied the country, on March 19, 1944, Horthy allowed the concentration and subsequent evacuation of the Jews, stopping the process only after the provinces had been "cleansed" of them; only after the Allies had landed in Europe; only when the liberation of the occupied countries had become a matter of a few months; and when the pressure to end the deportations intensified in the summer. Analyzing his stance, some of our friends believed that Horthy was not really pro-German; rather he had to act as if he were, in order to resist the Reich when Hungary's "vital interests were at stake." Most of them wished to believe that by accepting the anti-Jewish laws and pursuing anti-Jewish policies, Horthy was pacifying the demands of the Reich and was being able to avoid the German occupation of Hungary by doing so. Grasping my father's ambivalence in this matter, I listened to these arguments; sometimes I believed them, sometimes I did not.

In fact, I watched my father day and night, feeling that he was unsure of our future, unsure of our survival. At the same time, he, too, was obviously waiting for a miracle. And he was not alone. Obsessed by the fear of death and destruction, most of our friends and relatives maintained that the anti-Jewish measures in Hungary could have been even *more* humiliating, even *more* destructive, even *more* cruel, had the government not opposed the Germans. So it happened that slowly I became aware of a curious combination of tension and expectation that characterized most discussions among the Jews I knew in Hungary: they were optimistic sometimes, sometimes deeply pessimistic, but almost always they were fear-ridden regarding the future. I noted this tension, and it drove me crazy. What was going on? I could not answer my own questions. Neither could I understand my father, who tried to calm me down. Eventually, I started to pay attention to the news again and started to listen to people discussing politics and the Germans' assaults on the Jews.

One day, I overheard a tense discussion between my mother and father about the second anti-Jewish measures. To explain the problem, which I could not quite grasp, they told me that they were talking about the "expropriations of Jewish businesses." That meant, they said, that the law had legalized the "expropriation" of *our* pharmacy by the Hungarian government. At first I decided not to pay any attention to this news. I even remember that I promised myself not to ask them what the word *expropriation* meant. But then, hearing it over and over, and seeing the despair it stirred in everybody, I could not help but ask: "Expropriation? What is that?"

By then, my parents answered any question I asked.

"It means: to take possession of our pharmacy; to take it away from us," said my father.

"To take away our pharmacy? To steal it?"

"Yes. To steal it."

"But if they do *that, they* will be put in jail."

"No! The point is," my father said, "that they won't be put in jail. *This time, the criminals are in charge of the prisons, while decent people are the inmates.*"

Now I started to understand both what the word *expropriation* and the world of the "anti-Jewish measures" meant.

But I still could not quite understand what they meant for us. He then explained to me in plain words that we would lose our pharmacy, and that to earn an income, we might have to move from Békéscsaba.

What? We would have to go away and leave behind my friends, my school, my life?

"But why would we have to do this?" I felt powerless and angry, watching the expressions of sadness (which I knew already) and humiliation (which I had just started to recognize) change his face. And again and again, I clashed against his often repeated, incomprehensible answer:

"Because we are Jews."

But what does that mean? Why could we not be Jews? Whom did we harm? And who has the right to punish us? Were we not good people? Very good people? I had never seen or heard about anybody as good as my father and mother. They spoke to me all the time about the importance of caring for others; of understanding others; of the role of friendship; of helping those in need; of the need for sympathy and love; and of the importance of music and beautiful poetry in the world. I knew that they helped others with loving care, as did my grandparents on both sides: giving money, food, advice, jobs, and love to friends, relatives, and strangers. Who can force us to give up our pharmacy? And who can force us to move? But I was told that *they* could, because *they* were in power. And soon, I realized that we had started to lose the ground on which we stood, that we were not free anymore. We had to obey *them*. My father of all people had to obey thieves!

And again, I noticed that he hid his despair. My mother, on the other hand, showed it openly. In fact, she could not stand against the storm. She started to lose control. She felt threatened by the uncertainty of our future, crying out again and again:

"We'll lose our home! We'll lose our home for the *second* time!"

Poor Mother! She felt that our move from her hometown Subotica (Szabadka in Hungarian) to Békéscsaba had been her first "loss of home." But I knew even then that it was not. Clearly, as my father explained it, during the Depression many people had had to move from one place to another and try to make a living. Just like them, my parents had moved. Leaving Subotica, they had landed in Békéscsaba. Although this move had separated my mother from her family, she had not been singled out or humiliated, her belongings had not been expropriated, and she had not been chased away from the country of her birth. My parents had left of their own free will.

Sometime in the early summer of 1941, I formulated the difference: "We are not homeless," I told Iván. "Hanna is."

Soon my parents resolved to move from Békéscsaba to Budapest, where, luckily, my father had a chance to create a new life. Of course, a glance into the political developments of the time must have erased everybody's optimism. For the moment, however, my parents hoped to stay secure, at least for a while, at least economically.

3

PAST AND PRESENT

Thinking back to this period in our life, I remember that my mother suddenly felt the urge to tell me about her life and family, both of which, she said, she wanted me to know about now, because—and she looked at me crying—nobody can foresee the future. Hence, she said, I must know about the past, so that I could speak to my children about Szabadka, the town she was from, and about her relatives. Why did she say that? Why would my children have to *remember* her family? Would they not *know* them? Apparently she was not sure.

Today I understand the reason for her despair. First of all, she was lonely in Békéscsaba. She was living in a new milieu, bereft of her family and friends. Aware of the responsibility for her two children, her husband, and her new life, she could not deal with the threat the combination of the expanding Reich and the Hungarian Right posed. While my father pretended to be strong most of the time, she could not do so. In fact, she just could not deal with the growing anti-Semitism spreading over all aspects of Hungarian life, or with the nerve-racking rumors circulating in the city about the atrocities the Germans were committing against the Jews. She was scared. In fact, she lived in constant fear, lacking the means to suppress her recognition of the danger. Often she cried when she kissed me, pressing my hands or hugging me desperately while we talked. There can be no doubt that she told me much about the past, not only of her childhood but also of the mass murder of the Jews and the pogroms in Poland-Russia over the ages, claiming that she saw those murders essentially connected to the new persecution we were now hearing about every day. At times she was raging, at others, she just cried desperately. Sometimes she told me that all of this might be repeated in the future. I shuddered on hearing this.

But she also told me stories about her family in the darkening winter and spring afternoons, holding my hand firmly in hers. It was, I think, in 1941 that she started to come to my room and tell me these tales. I listened. In fact, I loved her stories. She talked to me about my grandmother, whose death, at the age of fifty-six, my mother forever mourned, and about my grandfather, a tall, elegant, well-spoken gentleman, white-haired and blue-eyed, whom she adored. She recounted stories about her brother, Uncle Imre, who was a pharmacist just like my grandfather, and Imre's wife, Cicus, yet another pharmacist in the family. The couple had two children, Éva and Gyurika (George), of whom she was very proud. And she told me both moving and funny stories about her three sisters: Anni, a redhead, with green eyes and freckles, who knew myths and legends, and much of Hungarian poetry by heart; Böske, blond, blue-eyed, and very intelligent, she was the fourth pharmacist in the family. She married the dentist József Kornél. The couple's son, Laci, a blond, chubby boy, was my mother's favorite. Ila, her third sister, had raven-dark hair, big brown eyes, and dark skin. She married Sándor Frank, a lawyer, and the new family moved to Hungary. Ila was also a brilliant cymbal player, but she had stopped practicing after she obtained her diploma at the Franz Liszt Music Academy in Budapest. Later on, I thought about the fact that my mother did not tell me why she stopped, and I did not ask. Still, every day, I eagerly awaited her new stories about my aunts, uncles, and cousins, each of whom I greatly enjoyed. And while I was looking into her large gray-green eyes as she spoke, her beautifully shaped noble face, framed by heavy, dark-blond hair, I saw that she was constantly struggling against her tears. She missed her relatives so much.

Despite these ties, however, or perhaps because of them, there were some deep-seated tensions within her family. Having had an exceptionally beautiful, sweetly flowing alto voice, my mother, Margit, had not only trained for many years to become an opera singer, but she had been encouraged to apply for a scholarship at the Budapest Opera, which meant that she had been moving toward the first step necessary at the time for starting a career as a young Hungarian singer. My grandfather, an old-fashioned gentleman, who grew up in a small nineteenth-century Jewish community, did not approve of her future as an opera singer, however. He felt that moving to Budapest by herself in case she was selected, working with and living in the milieu of artists and singers, might be devastating to the life and future of his lovely, sensitive, and vulnerable daughter, opening her up to "unspeakable dangers." As she told me the story, he did not have to fight hard against her will: she had indeed been unprepared to live apart from him and the rest of her family. In fact, she said, without her father's and siblings' approval, separation from them would have been unbearably difficult for her. Refusing to apply for her scholarship, my mother remained in Szabadka, although she would not have been the first one in her family to move away and achieve enormous success in the field of music. Her uncle, Jenő Adorján, had done so years before, concertizing all over Europe and becoming the first violinist of the Düsseldorf Opera. And her cousin, Gábor Fenyves, too, had left his home and family. He became a conductor and pianist in Minneapolis, in the United States. But they were men, who were allowed, in fact encouraged, to be independent, while women were not—and my mother had neither the strength nor the will to break the barriers.

Had she ever regretted her decision to turn away from the doors of the Budapest Opera? She must have. She was crying bitterly when she told me the story in Békéscsaba for the first time, and in 1964, in Dallas, Texas, when she referred to it for the last time. Still, despite her heartache, music remained for her a major source of delight. She would sing all day, beautifully: songs by Schubert, Schumann, and Brahms, Hungarian folk songs, and operatic arias. Her voice was mellow and smooth, and it was she who taught me how to make the piano sing.

She never blamed her father for her decision, or the rest of her family.

She married my father in Budapest in 1928. The couple moved to Subotica and led a very happy life there, with my father becoming an integral part of her family. They loved him, and he worked hard in my grandfather's pharmacy. After a while, my parents decided to move back to Hungary.

Yet Subotica was the town in which my mother grew up, a town she loved, a town where my grandfather had established himself successfully in the early 1900s. Originally a Hungarian city, placed in southern Hungary, Szabadka was renamed Subotica when it was annexed by Yugoslavia in 1919. This change took place after World War I, when the map of Europe was redrawn under the directions of the Peace Treaty of Versailles, which reshaped Germany, and the Peace Treaty of Trianon, dissolving the Austro-Hungarian monarchy and placing under foreign rule more than three million Hungarians. Despite obvious political tensions as a result of these changes, my mother told me then, and later again and again, that her family had continued to live with a sense of security, happiness, and satisfaction in Szabadka. My father's presence and our arrival only intensified their thriving.

As I understood much later, however, awareness of the past, politically and culturally, had remained part of Hungary's common consciousness, and so too had not only World War I and its hundreds of thousands of dead but also the loss of two-thirds of the country's territory and the loss of one-third of its population, living now under a foreign government. Indeed, enrolling in elementary school, I heard every single day about the Treaty of Trianon that had destroyed Greater Hungary. To demonstrate our awareness of what had happened, what the Allies had done to us, and how deeply and desperately we hoped for the return of justice one day, we prayed every morning in the Jewish day school for a change in the Hungarian political status quo, as did every Hungarian schoolchild in every other Hungarian school, and every Hungarian at every single national gathering in the country:

I believe in a God;
I believe in a homeland;
I believe in a divine, eternal justice;
I believe in the resurrection of Hungary.
Amen.

Even before I went to elementary school, it was explained to me that this prayer revolved around nothing less than the pain the Hungarian people had suffered because of the unjust Trianon peace treaty and their faith in and hope for the restoration of Hungary's thousand-year-old borders. And while my mother never ceased to speak about the "terrible injustice" this treaty had inflicted on the nation, my father pointed again and again to the neglect, even notorious oppression at times, of the Romanian and Slavic minorities in the Austro-Hungarian Empire.

My mother, however, allowed no criticism of the monarchy. Describing Szabadka as a traditionally Hungarian city, she explained to me what she saw as the essence of the problem the victors of World War I had created: "We must see and feel what has happened: our homeland, a thousand-year-old country, has been destroyed! Restoration must come in the near future to correct the ruination of this ancient kingdom, and remove the onus placed upon us by the Allies, claiming that Hungary was responsible for World War I."

She often mentioned this to me over the years, neglecting to call my attention to the anti-Semitic rightist parties' claim, according to which this treaty could have been carried out only because the Jews had betrayed Hungary (similar to what the German people were told about their "stab in the back")!

Again and again I heard the same anguish-laden history lesson in school: that Hungary was condemned to suffer the consequences of the cruel Treaty of Trianon.

It is a well-known fact that most Hungarian Jews were Hungarian patriots above all else. Although the political crisis created by the Trianon treaty did not subside for decades, in their private lives most families tried to adjust to the new circumstances, living their lives, caring for their loved ones, working hard, and saving for the future. We lived in a big house in Szabadka, in my mother's large, extended family dwelling. Having two children of their own, my parents felt happy, safe, and comfortable. Still, when in the early 1930s the Depression cut across the countries of the world, it caused the collapse of the Yugoslav economy as well. For years, my mother told me, she and my father were worried about the possibility of a moratorium imposed upon foreign accounts in Yugoslav banks, which could mean the loss of their savings. After a while, they became convinced of the necessity of moving their bank account back to Hungary. They hoped to invest their money in a Hungarian pharmacy, so that inflation would not further devalue their capital. They found one for sale, paid for it with cash, and we moved to Békéscsaba. At this point of her tale, whenever my mother recounted this story, she would cry bitterly. There can be no doubt, moving away from Szabadka meant giving up her family, her home, her love, and her security. She was and remained forever deeply wounded by the sudden and brutal separation from her father and from the rest of her siblings.

4

A DREAM DISRUPTED

The new pharmacy in Békéscsaba did quite well, although not as well as it could have, not as well as my parents had hoped.

"What can I do?" my father asked my mother once. They thought I was outside, but I was hiding under the table. His face was pale, his eyes glistened with tears, but he knew that there was no answer to the question. "The truth of the matter is that this pharmacy I love so much is recommended to their patients in the area neither by the Christian private doctors nor by the hospital doctors," he said.

There were reasons, of course, for such expressions of hatred, which took me years to understand. My father was charming, caring, and very intelligent, not only adored by us but by everybody else who met him. In addition, he was an excellent businessman and a highly gifted chemist who undertook major research experiments, inventing and producing several potent medications. Yet despite his personal charm, brilliance, and professional excellence, he could not fight the growing boycotts unleashed against the Jews in the mid-1930s in Hungary.

Indeed, finding its roots in age-old religious hatred, anti-Semitism still had enormous energy and resources in Hungary—as the Blood Libel trial at Tiszaeszlár at the end of the nineteenth century, accusing the Jews of drinking the blood of a Christian maiden, had demonstrated. This powerful, myth-based emotion did not disappear completely during the years of the country's rapid modernization. And after World War I, during the time of "new troubles" created by a Communist takeover and Trianon, it was ripe for explosion. In fact, as my parents observed, under the pressure of the lost war and the collapsing economy, anti-Jewish feelings intensified and intermingled with the radical Right's racist propaganda, blaming the Jews for the lost war as well as the Bolshevik Revolution and the Hungarian Communist government, while simultaneously advancing rumors about Jewish "profit" from the war and the growth of Jewish "financial capital." While becoming more restrained during the relatively stable years of 1922–28, anti-Jewish sentiments flamed up again in Hungary during the Depression.

"It was, in fact, under the impact of this new, catastrophic pressure," said my father, and as often as he spoke of this his face expressed shame and anguish, "that the old anti-Jewish sentiments were reincarnated in Hungary.

"Yes," he said, trying to be "objective," but even then I saw his anguish. "There was hunger, uncertainty, fear, and hatred. People were desperate. The food and coal lines multiplied in the streets; and with them arose the hostility against the 'foreigners' who 'caused the war' and 'brought Communism to Hungary.' The infamous *Numerus Clausus* law came again into effect," he added, "restricting to 5 percent the number of Jewish students at the country's universities."

Many years were to pass before he could tell me what this "rising hostility" had meant for our life. Reading books about it later, I understood that, indeed, accused of participation in the Communist rule in Hungary, masses of Jews had been killed by the Horthy-led army of the Right during the counterrevolution in 1919. In addition to this bloodshed, hundreds of Jewish students in Hungarian universities had been beaten up and crippled by blows. One of these students who had been attacked was my father, who had just returned from the war in the fall of 1918 after suffering on the front a head wound, from which he had almost died. Matriculating a year later at Budapest University, he was targeted after a chemistry lab session, beaten by a mob of "Awakening Hungarians"—an ultra-Right, anti-Semitic organization—and hurled down several flights of steep stone stairs leading from the doors of the university to the street, hitting his head again and again during the fall, till he hit the pavement.

Left lying on the sidewalk in a pool of blood, he was picked up by some of his friends, who saved his life by taking him to a nearby hospital.

These attacks subsided after a while, and the country started to recover from the war. But then came the Depression, and Hungary, like several other European countries of the time, had arrived at the brink of an economic collapse. With the help of its then prime minister, Gyula Gömbös, however, it slowly became successful in cooperating with the Third Reich. Indeed, as the first head of a foreign government to visit Hitler, in June 1933, Gömbös was instrumental in building up a flourishing economic exchange between Hungary and the Reich. In the process, the Hungarian economy became significantly stronger. At the same time, anti-Semitism in the country turned ever more vehement.

As I heard from my father over and over, a significant relationship developed between the German-friendly Hungarian government and the country's middle and upper classes, which were called upon to help "Christian business activities." Most of them joined the efforts of the government and the program of the Right radical political parties to reduce "Jewish presence and Jewish influence" in the economy. Hence my parents' desperate discussion regarding the drop of customers in our pharmacy. In fact, I can still hear the whispers of some of our friends and acquaintances, reporting to my father exchanges they witnessed among the town's "leading doctors and pharmacists," describing him as a Shylock who should not have the privilege of owning a pharmacy.

I looked at him the moment he spoke to my mother about these attacks and saw him standing in the kitchen, his eyes cast downward and his face bearing the same humiliation that changed his features years later as well, when he first told me about the fellow students beating him up at the university. No matter how he felt, however, the medical community did not change its mind over time. Although loved and highly appreciated by many in the Jewish community and outside of it as well, with his pharmacy eventually even having some success on its own, my father, as a professional, was mostly overlooked or outright sabotaged by the rest of Békéscsaba's medical community.

Still, even though he did not do as well as the rest of the "Christian pharmacists" (this is the phrase people used to describe themselves, which meant in the Hungarian context in the interwar period that they were *not* Jewish), he certainly made enough money for his family's modest daily needs. As for his belief in the future of humanity, he was deeply optimistic—so he said, at least—despite all the signs pointing toward the loss of reason in the world. In fact, he often spoke of his vision of an economic recovery in Europe and the end of the Depression. Whenever that came about, he thought, Hungary would become part of this new development, and, at that point, he believed, the country would not need the help of the Reich anymore; in which case, he suggested, a significant general improvement in Hungarian political and social life would take place.

But even when he spoke of his hope for a better life, for a more enlightened, more humane future, I felt that his beliefs did not match his horrendous fear of the Germans. It was only much later that I understood the contradiction: he was frightened, although he also had a strong sense of self-determination and an overwhelming drive for survival. As he admitted to me after the war, until 1944 he had lived with a conflicted consciousness. While he believed that war threats and violence would one day cease to influence the political landscape, he was also terribly concerned about the news coming from the Reich and felt directly threatened by the Germans. As early as 1934, he had considered leaving his father and siblings behind and emigrating with us to the United States, where he had had an excellent offer from a pharmaceutical firm. Moving there, he told me much later, he could have made a very good living, and we could have finally lived "as Jews, with our heads held up high," he said, "rather than lowered." But since my mother would never even consider leaving behind the continent where her father and the rest of her family lived, he kept on postponing any serious attempt at emigration until it was too late.

This was a mistake he never ceased to regret. For the economic-political partnership intensified between Hungary and the Third Reich in the mid-1930s, and the Hungarian ultra-Right achieved growing popularity. Then, with the promulgation of the first anti-Jewish law in May 1938, anti-Jewish agitation became part of the political scene. The first law against the Jews was soon followed by the second, which went into effect in May 1939. And it was the latter that promulgated the decree that the licenses held by Jews for the operation of pharmacies must be reduced. Ultimately, with the third anti-Jewish law adopted in the summer of 1941, my father's pharmacy became a liability. He decided to sell it. In fact, it had been his younger brother, Pali, a thirty-four-year-old lawyer, with dark brown, shiny eyes and a regularly carved, highly intelligent face, who lived in Békés, near Békéscsaba, who had convinced him to do so. Hammering slowly but persistently at the problem, Pali convinced first my father, then my mother, of the realities of the anti-Jewish measures, warning my parents of the future. Initially, they would not hear of selling.

"Why should I?" asked my father, outraged. "After all," he demanded, "have you forgotten that I was a silver-decorated lieutenant in World War I? Don't you know that I was exempt from all anti-Jewish measures?"

But as it turned out, he was not. Upon Pali's insistence, my parents started to face the threat and decided to move.

Luckily, the pharmacy was sold within two weeks—for half its value, though still a good price for a Jewish pharmacy—and we arrived in Budapest in the last days of August 1941. At this point, my parents invested the rest of their money in a bicycle shop my father started with his childhood friend Louis. Although by then Jews were not permitted to open new businesses, Louis was and remained exempt from these measures because he had been a gold-decorated hero and a first lieutenant in World War I. My father became his "silent partner" on a profit-sharing basis. The bicycle shop did well until the German occupation of March 19, 1944, when it was officially appropriated by the Hungarian state, its warehouse looted.

But poor Pali. Foreseeing his brother's future did not help him foresee his own: he was murdered just the same. There can be no doubt, however, that he had saved our lives. By moving to Budapest in 1941, we were not subjected to the expulsion and deportation of Békéscsaba's Jewish community to Auschwitz in the early summer of 1944, as was every single Jew in the city, including our friends and my classmates at the Jewish elementary school, each of whom was killed in Auschwitz-Birkenau.

5

CHANGES

"Hungary forever! Hurrah, hurrah, hurrah!"

Iván was beside himself. He ran through the kitchen when he heard that the Hungarian troops had arrived in the "Southern Region" (Délvidék in Hungarian), one of the regions of ancient Hungary that had been annexed to Yugoslavia by the Peace Treaty of Trianon in 1920. The troops arrived in April 1941. The Jews of Hungary had already suffered the terrible consequences of the two harsh and highly discriminatory anti-Jewish measures and had already known about both the ever-closer relationship between their country and the Reich and the German atrocities committed against the Jews in Europe. Yet most of them were still enthusiastic Hungarian patriots, concerned with the injustice that had destroyed their precious homeland in 1920. Thus most Jews, us included, participated in the general euphoria regarding Hitler's return to Hungary of the "Southern Region" including Szabadka, where Iván and I had been born, and where my mother had lived most of her life. With the return of these territories, Hungarians, including, of course, Hungarian Jews, felt that a major wrong had been remedied in the world. While I can no longer recall the reaction of my parents to these changes, I remember that Iván wrote a letter of celebration to my grandfather in Szabadka, expressing his admiration for the Hungarian army and his ardent wish to throw flowers on the paths of the Hungarian soldiers marching across the Bácska region. I also know that the Hungarian public, together with the Jewish community, including me and my classmates at my Jewish elementary school, exulted for days, rejoicing at the fulfillment of the Hungarian dream, celebrating the "resurrection" of Hungary.

It soon became clear, however, that we had a high price to pay for the generosity of the Germans; that, in fact, this newly "resurrected" Hungary did not bring unity, liberation, or freedom to all. At least, not to the Jews. In the first week of August 1941, my mother, Iván, and I visited Szabadka, without my father, who had to stay in the pharmacy. We did not go there on vacation, though. We went to be with my grandfather, who had suffered a stroke after his pharmacy was expropriated by the Hungarian state. My mother told me on the train that he was so sick he might not immediately recognize us.

It was unusual to arrive in Szabadka with no one waiting for us at the station. Taking a taxi, we drove to grandfather's house.

"Oh my God!" I called out when I saw him in bed. Recognizing us, he started to cry. For that I was not prepared. Unshaven, pale, his gaze fixed on the ceiling, his always elegantly groomed white hair drenched with sweat and sticking to his forehead, he had aged beyond recognition.

"Shhhhhh," said my aunt Anni, her face phosphorescently pale, her heavily veined hands trembling, as she watched him from a chair. She could not get up to kiss us; she merely waved when we arrived, tears running down her face. Likewise, the rest of the family cried.

"He is terribly, terribly sick," whispered my mother. She stroked my hair. "Losing his license, he lost his pharmacy. It simply was taken away from him."

By then I fully understood the meaning of the word *expropriation*.

In fact, what happened to Grandfather was the direct outcome of the German-Hungarian agreement that returned to Hungary some of the territories annexed to Yugoslavia in 1920. This was the Reich's "reward" for the country's participation in the military operation against Yugoslavia. In this way, Subotica became Szabadka, a Hungarian city again, where Hungarian laws ruled, among them, of course, the two sets of anti-Jewish measures. Going into effect as soon as the change of administration took place, these measures forced the Jews out of their state jobs altogether, while most of them also lost their businesses. These changes brought great confusion and despair to the Jewish community. The Jews of "Trianon Hungary" had a bit more time for adjustment, while those of the "Southern Region" were turned into pariahs within a few months. As our relatives and my parents' best friends reported, a few of the Yugoslav-Hungarian Jews committed suicide, a few moved to Budapest, and a few tried to escape to other countries. Most stayed, however, and, like the rest of the country's Jews, became impoverished. In spring 1944, their status and future essentially changed: they were placed into ghettos and deported to Auschwitz.

Caught up in the storm, my grandfather could not deal with the physical and emotional blows he received. Eighty years old, kicked out of the pharmacy he had cultivated for almost fifty years, deprived of his work, his pride, his achievement, he felt he had arrived at the end of his life. It was heartrending to see him cry in anguish. My mother decided to stay in Szabadka for a while, hoping to help him make up his mind regarding the future. She, in fact, tried to convince him to move to Budapest rather than stay in Szabadka, where he would have to see, even be confronted with, his spectacularly beautiful "expropriated" pharmacy every day, as soon as he walked toward the center of town. For there could be no doubt, his pharmacy had been an integral part of one of "greater Hungary's" most beautiful, majolica-decorated city halls, located in the major plaza of Szabadka. Budapest, on the other hand, was neutral territory. No pharmacy and no memories would remind him of the past. Besides, we too were in the process of moving there within the next few weeks and so, she thought, we could be together all the time, going to theater and concerts, taking long walks, and visiting one another. Arguing back and forth, my mother and her siblings agreed that Grandfather would buy, and move into, a house in Budapest with his oldest daughter, my mother's sister Anni, who shared the family house with him in Szabadka, and who was more than happy to follow him to the capital.

Hearing this, I was overjoyed! For I loved Grandfather and found Anni to be the best, nicest, and sweetest person in the world. I also felt great sorrow for her because she had been crippled by tuberculosis of the bone from the hip down ever since her childhood, and could walk only with the help of two canes. Yet her constant anguish notwithstanding, she was generous, witty, gracious, intelligent, warm-hearted, and loving. She never married, however. She simply stayed with her father throughout her life. At the same time, she loved her nephews and nieces, including me. She read to me, played with me, and recounted to me almost as many beautiful fairy tales as Erzsi. I enjoyed being around her, and I loved my grandfather as well. I could not wait for their move to Budapest! And when they arrived in the fall of 1941, I considered their presence as a kind of compensation for my lost friends, Márta and Juti, who stayed in Békéscsaba, while we moved to the capital.

By the time we left Szabadka in the middle of August 1941, Grandfather had recovered somewhat from his stroke. A couple of months later, he moved to Budapest with Anni. Spending much time with us, they seemed to adjust quite well to their new surroundings. But despite the attempts of Anni and my mother to help Grandfather forget the terrible loss of his pharmacy and his home in Szabadka, he could not recover from the trauma. Not even our love could save him from a second stroke. Grandfather Bertalan died in December 1942, in Budapest. His funeral was in Szabadka. Nor did Anni want to stay in the capital. She moved back to her hometown, the place where she had lived throughout her life.

But the world changed in Hungary during the weeks we had spent in Szabadka. Upon our return to Békéscsaba, we were met by my father at the train station. He was deeply depressed. It had happened in the course of the past few days, he said, that Hanna and her mother disappeared, together with some other Jews from Békéscsaba and elsewhere. Defined as "alien Jews," they had been rounded up and sent to camps with thousands of other "alien Jews," as an employee of the Jewish Federation told him. My father did not know what all of this meant. We heard later from some of our friends that Hanna's grandparents had attempted to find an exemption for their daughter and grandchild, but they could not. It did not matter that Hanna's mother had been born and lived in Hungary until she turned twenty-four, or that her parents were Hungarians who had never left Hungary. Hanna had been born in Poland, and her mother had married a Pole. They counted now as "foreign Jews" and were rounded up just the same.

Several months passed after their roundup before my parents heard about the real fate of these people. At first, my father and mother believed and accepted, as did most Hungarian Jews, that this group of "aliens" (many of whom were Hungarians who for some reason or another could not produce Hungarian birth certificates or certificates of residency), about 16,000 to 18,000 Jews, would be moved to "safe camps," where they would stay until the end of the war. But then, in the late fall of 1941, unexpectedly, a few of these "alien Jews" returned to Hungary. One of them had appeared in Békéscsaba, making it immediately clear that *where* he had been and *what* he had witnessed did not square with what the rest of the Hungarian Jews had been told about the group. As a matter of fact, he said, the so-called foreign Jews had not been taken to "safe camps." Quite the contrary. Entrained in Hungary, they had been "transferred" across the Hungarian border. There they had found themselves among new, large groups of Jews, all of whom had been handed over to the Germans. Marched to an area near Kemenets-Podolsk in the Ukraine, these groups were machine-gunned into mass graves by SS and Wehrmacht troops and their helpers, the Ukrainian militia, in addition to a Hungarian sapper platoon. A few fled. The rest, however, were killed.

My God! Poor Hanna. Once had not been enough: she was taken to the "marketplace" for a second time. But this time she did not escape. As for the handful of Jews who did, some of them feigned being dead and managed to flee during the night from the mass graves. A few of them even made their way back to Hungary, despite the cold, hunger, and destruction, recounting what had happened to the rest of the community.

When in the late fall of 1941 my parents heard the truth about the "foreign Jews," as they told me later, they did everything in their power to cover it up so that I would not hear about Hanna's murder. They were successful, because by then we were living in Budapest and our friends did not know the family; probably, most of them did not even know the fate of the "foreign Jews" either. In the winter of 1945, after liberation and our march across the country from Budapest to Békéscsaba to escape starvation, my parents decided to tell me about the massacre; otherwise, they feared, I might hear about it from someone else. But to decide is one thing and to act upon it is another: in the end, they did not tell me. As they later admitted, they still felt incapable of talking to me about it.

By late February, early March 1945, a few surviving deportees returned to Békéscsaba. Some of them we knew. Being present at their discussions with my parents, I understood that all of my friends had been murdered in Auschwitz upon arrival. But to me, Hanna was another case. After all, I had been told a long time ago that the "foreign Jews" had been taken to a "safe camp." Hence, I was waiting for her throughout the winter and the spring of 1945. I wanted to apologize for having avoided her, to explain that I loved her deeply, that I had learned a great deal from her, and that I wanted to be her best friend forever. Several times a week I visited the house where she once lived with her mother and grandparents. But after the deportation of her grandparents, some other people moved into that house, and they knew nothing of Hanna's family. Still I waited for her. Weeks went by. Months. We moved back to Budapest. I was still waiting for her. I believed she somehow got to Russia, but that she would return. I was wrong; she never did. Later, my father said that most Jews, when they first heard others speaking about the rounding up and entrainment of the "alien Jews" in the summer of 1941, were inclined to believe that "giving up the foreigners" was a sacrifice the Hungarian government "had to make" in order to "save the rest of the Hungarian Jewish community." But as I found out much later, the Hungarian government made no "sacrifice" whatsoever. Just the opposite was true. It was the Hungarian National Central Alien Control Office, under the control of the Hungarian Ministry of the Interior, that *suggested* and *carried out* the "transfer." In other words, what was behind the deportation and killing of the "alien Jews," among them my friend Hanna, involved a Hungarian political decision.

6

ERZSI

Back in the early summer of 1941, when I first became aware of my parents' decision to move to Budapest, I felt terribly sad. To say farewell to Békéscsaba meant giving up my best friends, Márta and Juti, and with them to leave behind our games, our plays, my whole life. But there was someone else from whom I knew I could not and would not want to part, someone without whom I could not imagine my life. This person was Erzsi. Small, thin, with light brown hair, a heart-shaped face, emerald eyes, and round lips, Erzsi was twenty-three years old. She was our nanny, our playmate; in fact, she was the good fairy in our life. Since Erzsi's parents lived in Békéscsaba, I feared they would never let her come to Budapest and live with us. And what was worse, I believed, neither would she wish to do anything against their will.

They had sent her to work when she was a little girl, thirteen years of age, that's true. But they had had to. Her father was unemployed and her mother barely made ends meet. In fact, the wages Mr. Fajó earned as an occasional worker and Mrs. Fajó as a washerwoman were not enough to support their family. Erzsi helped, and so did her younger sister, Dóra. But even ten years later, Erzsi still felt responsible for her family, believing that she must support them and would always support them, with all her love and all her might and all her will. She spoke to me often about this. One night, I remember, after spinning out one of her magical fairy tales, she switched her voice to tell me *true* stories, describing her home life, including her mother's anguish, their fight against poverty and starvation, and their struggle against suffering and death. Horrified, I listened to these stories of pain. Also, by then, I knew already about my parents' plan to move to Budapest. I thought I would ask her. Searching her face with my eyes, I did so directly: What would she do if we had to move? She answered me slowly, her face pale, her lips barely moving: Of course, she would always send money to her parents and visit them as often as possible, she said. But no matter what, she would come with us to the end of the world, because she could never leave us or live without us. She never did.

When she started to work in my father's pharmacy, Erzsébet (Erzsi) Fajó had just completed sixth grade with an A in every subject on her report card. Shortly after her school ended in June of that year, she was told by her parents that she could not go to middle school in the fall, as she hoped, because they needed her financial help. At that time, the Hungarian state required only six years of schooling. Erzsi had completed her last year, and now she had to work and earn money.

Erzsi's parents came from Slovakia, but had lived in Hungary for a long time, as had millions of other minorities—some for years or decades, others for centuries or longer. The Fajós had eight children. Starting out his work in Békéscsaba, Erzsi's father was a bricklayer. But only before World War I, Erzsi said, had he been able to earn wages doing construction work, because during the war years, construction shut down completely in the country. As Erzsi told me, Mr. Fajó and his wife took whatever work they could get: cleaning houses, washing clothes, packing boxes in warehouses, and cooking meals. But it was during World War I, at the time of catastrophic upheavals, hunger, and unemployment, that Mr. Fajó became interested in the workers' unionization programs and political activism. And after the war, during the Communist takeover in Hungary in 1919, he even became a member of the Communist Party. But the rule of the Communist Party and the Communist government was short-lived in Hungary. The leadership failed and the counterrevolution, under the leadership of Admiral Horthy, won. The Communists were chased away or killed. In addition, everyone who joined or sympathized with them was persecuted by Horthy's new justice system. In fact, the right-wing police and the notoriously brutal gendarmerie constantly spied on, searched for, and punished those who were involved then or before with the political Left. As my father and Erzsi later recounted, while executing, torturing, and locking up people in prisons, the system had made sure that those who were members of the Communist Party would never again land a job. Thus Mr. Fajó remained unemployed for the rest of his life. And, Erzsi admitted, he became increasingly more difficult, reaching for the bottle, beating up his children and his wife, all of whom were afraid of him. Reacting to her husband's behavior, Mrs. Fajó kept on working ever harder: washing clothes, cleaning people's houses and businesses. Still, she could not support the family by herself. Her two older daughters married and had babies of their own, hoping to do better than their parents, but they never did. Life was hard in Hungary during the inter-war period, with millions of people living in poverty. Erzsi's younger brother passed away at the age of six, and her older one died of a tetanus infection, which he contracted in a mill where he worked, she told me, crying. The next son of the Fajós drowned in the Kőrös River, while the youngest was, and remained for the time being, like his father, unem-ployed. Both younger girls, Erzsi and Dóra, had to pitch in and help support themselves and their family.

Erzsi was offered up to my parents by her mother as a delivery girl in the pharmacy soon after we arrived in Békéscsaba. A couple of days after she started to work there, she met Iván, then a little boy, and me, barely a month old. Falling immediately in love with her, Iván did not want to part from the best playmate he ever had; he would not let her go or even leave our apartment. And as my parents had to listen to his pas-sionate arguments, they became willing to make some accommodations and let Erzsi spend a few hours a day with us, away from the pharmacy. After a week, however, Iván objected. He would not hear of just a few hours: he demanded Erzsi as a playmate for the entire day. My parents did not object. Erzsi moved in and lived with us, like a sister, for the years to come. Burdened by her childhood, overshadowed by poverty,

quarrels, violence, and abuse at home, she suddenly landed in a fairy-
tale world of children and adults who loved her, and who in fact encouraged her to become a child again and play day and night with everything
she wanted, in whatever ways she imagined. She drew pictures with us,
read to us, sang with us, played games and make-believe with us. She
acted out stories for us and created both dramatic and comic characters
with us, inventing tales and conjuring up events about them. In fact, she
became our friend and companion with a passion that shaped our life.
We adored her.

Our happiness notwithstanding, before my fifth birthday our idyll
with Erzsi suddenly threatened to come to an end. My mother, who
had grown up in a German-speaking environment and admired German art and culture, as most Hungarian Jews had, felt that the time
was ripe for us to learn to speak German as well. In this respect, she
was not held back by the bad news from Germany. Despite Hitler and
the Nazis, she believed in the value of speaking German, reading German literature, listening to German music, and surrounding our life
with German culture. Despite the horror stories, she decided to hire a
nanny whose mother tongue was German, and let Erzsi go back to the
pharmacy. I cried and cried. Iván was terribly angry, planning several
ways of revenge.

The day before the new nanny arrived, he made a promise to Erzsi:
"I will never allow the new girl to come to the bathroom while I am
taking a shower. You, however, may always see me naked, whenever
you wish."

Erzsi assured him she would want to do that often.

Whatever the new nanny (Kamilla was her name) could or could
not see, she could certainly not stand the torture Iván inflicted on her
every day. And then, encouraged by his behavior, I, too, boycotted her
rules and refused to abide by her requests. This we did, using all the
means we had, and whenever we could. After swallowing the bitter pill
for only two months, Kamilla left.

We had five nannies in one year, with each desperately wanting to leave after a few weeks. At this point, my parents gave up their plan. My mother took over our instruction in German, and Erzsi moved back from the pharmacy to the nursery, where she stayed with us until we moved from Békéscsaba to Budapest in the early fall of 1941.

7

OPTIONS

As time went by, it was more and more obvious that school had lost its importance in my life, while music would become of the most essential, shaping significance. I became serious about playing the piano. From the age of eight, I practiced two to three hours every day and listened to music all the time. I even played chamber music with my father's quartet on Sunday afternoons, enjoying our performances tremendously. And if, after a while, the thought of moving to Budapest started to seem bearable to me, it was so not only because I knew by then that Erzsi, Anni, and Grandfather would live there as well, but also because my father found a teacher for me in the capital, one of the greatest pianists of the time in Hungary: György (Gyuri) Faragó, a dashingly attractive young man, with blond curly hair, blue eyes, and a beautifully shaped, intelligent face. He had won the first prize in the International Piano Competition of Luxemburg a few years before. We listened to his recordings all the time and, whenever we traveled to Budapest, we went to his concerts as well.

Despite my new interest developing beyond the world of Békéscsaba, saying farewell to Márta and Juti was very difficult. I felt a terrible emptiness without them and could not imagine that anyone could ever substitute for them, that I could ever forget our relationship or find anything comparable to it. Hoping to stay close and continue our friendship, we decided to visit one another regularly in the future. Despite our best intentions, however, we met just once more in our lives: when I spent two weeks in Békéscsaba in July 1942. During the summer of

1943, we missed seeing each other altogether. I went to the mountains with my mother, and both of them went visiting relatives. Unbeknownst to all of us, however, this was our last chance to be together. On March 19, 1944, the Germans occupied Hungary, and from that time on, each of us ran for her life.

Of course, in August–September 1941, we did not know what was in the making. Although the news of the Germans' torture and massacres of the Jews had been known in Hungary for years, the scope and inevitability of the Final Solution were not yet recognized by most people. While Jews like my parents had a sense of the impending catastrophe, their concerns and visions, especially those of my father, especially before my uncle's murder on the front, were, I believe, suppressed most of the time in order to live and fulfill the task of raising, supporting, nourishing, and teaching their children, whose everyday lives demanded active and caring parents.

After the three of us returned from Szabadka in the late summer of 1941, my parents placed us in a boarding school in Budapest, while they started to prepare for our move. They were looking forward to the good and productive life they hoped to secure for us in the capital. My mother was now happy as well. Knowing that my grandfather and Anni would be near us, she looked forward to our life in the city. Iván and I arrived there within two weeks, moving to 10 Abonyi Street, across from the Jewish high school, a red-stone building with an outstanding library and a first-class faculty. Erzsi, on the other hand, took a small apartment in Buda, close to her workplace. She got a job in the bicycle shop belonging to my father and his friend Louis, and we saw her only on Sundays. That was hard. But when she came, we played with one another as passionately and as happily as we used to play in Békéscsaba.

The rumors of the brutal treatment of the Jews on the Soviet front would not subside, however. In fact, we heard about the anguish of the labor servicemen again and again, and became aware of the drafting and service on the front of several of my schoolmates' fathers. After a while, people started to whisper about mass shootings of children, men, and women into pits in the Ukraine. I was horrified. Suddenly Budapest was buzzing with these stories. At this point, I could not avoid hearing them, nor could my parents hide them from me. Then, in January–February 1942, we started to hear terrible news from Hungarian-occupied Yugoslavia. At first I ran out of the room whenever I heard people speaking about it, but there was no escape. Wherever two Jews met, they spoke of this event. Soon the bloodbath became known as "the massacre at Ujvidék" ("Novisad" in Serbo-Croatian). This was not a German undertaking, however. Hungarian military troops, together with units of the Hungarian gendarmerie, systematically mowed down masses of Jews and Serbs, together with their families, children and the aged alike. Soon we learned the details of this event. After a series of massive roundup operations, lasting for weeks, 1,000 Jewish men, women, and children, and 2,000 Serbs, family upon family, were driven to the banks of the Duna and Tisza rivers, stripped of their clothes, and forced to stand naked in freezing weather, sometimes for hours, before they were shot into the ice-covered water that had just been shattered by cannon fire. My parents were shaken. Having lived for many years in the region, both of them had friends and acquaintances among the victims, for whom they mourned the rest of their lives. They also had friends among those who were taken to court a few months later, identified and convicted as Communist traitors or as spies for the Allies, and executed in Szabadka. These were, however, innocent people, as innocent of political conspiracy as was anybody else. They were killed for no reason other than that they were Jewish. There could be no doubt, the war against the Jews had come closer to us, touching upon our lives directly.

In fact, to deny the danger in which we lived was no longer possible. Young men identified as Jews started to disappear. More and more were drafted into the labor service and taken to the Ukrainian front, where most of them were murdered. As I learned much later, out of the 50,000 Jewish men drafted between 1941 and 1943, 42,000 lost their lives. And they were killed not by bombs, shelling, or even friendly fire, but by the murderous treatment of the Hungarian armed forces, who tortured and starved the Jewish servicemen. Besides my uncle Pali, several of my friends' fathers, including my father's friends, colleagues, and chamber music partners, were drafted into labor service. None of them returned.

"How come nobody saved them?" asked Erzsi once, when she overheard my parents' discussion of the fate of the labor servicemen on the front.

"Who could have saved them?" I turned back the question.

"I think I could," she replied.

I stopped breathing for a second: "How?"

She did not answer; she was thinking.

That night I dreamed of angels: they looked very strange, though. Some were small, some were tiny, some were large; some were blond, some were dark, some were redheads; some had emerald eyes and some had brown. But each of them had Erzsi's face.

8

PALI

The year 1941 expired; 1942 stepped into its place. We listened to the BBC every day. Iván and my father followed the war on the map, and they were very optimistic.

"There can be no doubt," said my father, "the Russians are winning on the Eastern front, and soon the Americans will land in France or Italy."

I can still hear my mother's whisper to Erzsi: "Perhaps it won't last forever? Perhaps we'll survive despite everything? Perhaps it won't get much worse before it gets better?"

Then, suddenly, our world was shaken by an event that has forever impaired our lives: the draft of Pali into labor service on the front.

In the fall of 1942, my father fell ill. Nothing terribly complicated, just an inflammation of the kidneys, but he was bedridden for a while. Pali came to visit him, undertaking a four-hour train trip from Békés to Budapest. He was always worried about my father. But now he seemed to be even more concerned. And this was no coincidence. They had lost their mother when my father was sixteen and Pali seven years old. Three years later, their older brother committed suicide (for reasons that we have never known). Living with a sense of tragedy and death, Pali and my father grew enormously close to one another as children, and they remained close and loving brothers throughout their lives. Graduating from law school, Pali wanted to be near my father, so he moved to Békés, a town seven miles from Békéscsaba. He opened his own law firm there. The pair spent much time together, discussing books, politics, and family, playing chamber music, enjoying their lives and each other. Pali visited us at least twice a week. Often we lit up every room in the house, just for him to see from afar that we were at home, waiting for him.

He and my father adored their sister, Lulu, too, a highly intelligent woman; she had dark hair, big brown eyes, and a beautiful face. She was a pianist who lived in Sopron, a town near the Austrian border. The siblings always found occasions to visit one another. Then, suddenly, Lulu's husband, Béla, died in his late thirties of an untreated kidney disease, leaving his wife and two young sons behind. Soon after, my paternal grandfather died, a loss that shook Pali to the core. Afterward, he became even more concerned about my father. Hearing now that he was sick, Pali mounted the train early in the morning just to see him for a few hours—for he wanted to go back the same day, he said. I met him at noon when I came home from school, throwing myself into his arms. I had not seen him for a long time!

"Please stay," I begged him.

No, he could not stay, he said, smiling vaguely. He just wanted to see my father and us for a short while. Now that he had done so and understood that everything was OK, he wanted to leave and finish the work he had to complete for a client by the end of the week.

"Bye-bye, old boy," he hugged my father. "I hope to see you soon."

But he never saw him again. For in the pocket of Pali's striped, gray trousers hid his death sentence: his draft card, which, as his wife, Margit, told us later, he "wouldn't want to discuss with Laci" (my father), because he did not want to "harm" or "upset" him. This was a decision for which he and all of us had to pay a horrific price. It was October 1942.

After visiting my father and taking the train home, Pali knew that he had to appear next morning at the barracks that the draft card had specified, and he knew that from there, he would be taken to the front. As we learned much later, during his stay at our house in Budapest, his wife, Margit, was washing, ironing, packing, and baking to prepare his backpack for the journey. Nine months pregnant, she had a hard day, not only because she had to think through her life, which would now have to go on without her husband, probably for a long, long time (she did not know, of course, that it was forever), but also because she had to make immediate plans for the future. She knew that she would have to keep her full-time work as a visiting nurse in order to earn enough money to support both their two-year-old daughter, Magdi, and the baby, Margit, she was pregnant with. Despite the fact that she came from a well-to-do family with a name that, owing to Hungary's semifeudal system, enabled most of its members to land work in leading government and military positions, she saw little hope in turning to them for help. They were already quite angry at her for marrying a Jew. Obviously, however gifted, intelligent, and loving, a Jew was surely not on the wish list of most Hungarian-Christian families at the time. Margit had serious disputes with her mother and siblings regarding her marriage. As a result, she dared not ask any of her influential and powerful relatives to help change Pali's draft card from one barracks to another, or from service at the front to service at home, for the kind of "illegal" help that could have nonetheless stopped the machinery of death that catapulted poor Pali to the front.

It was 7:00 P.M. when he arrived at home. And next morning at 5:00 A.M., he left the house, to which he would never return. It took two weeks before my father's health improved. Only then did he receive Pali's farewell card that Margit finally had the courage to send him; only then did he learn from her what had played itself out during the time he was sick. But it was too late. While my father had regained his health, Pali faced torture and death. My father knew this, and he was heartbroken. Well informed and well connected, he was aware of the torture unleashed against the labor servicemen. Trying to move everyone he knew, bribing high-ranking, corrupt government employees and high-ranking, corrupt military personnel, he finally managed to get Pali's discharge from duty. But it was too late. The communication carrying the discharge arrived at its destination a day *after* Pali had been "lost in action."

Year after year would pass, and although my father knew about the fate of the servicemen, he never ceased to search for people who had survived in Pali's labor-service company, former servicemen or guards alike. This ongoing search brought him nothing, however, but hurtful, unsatisfactory encounters. While he found a few former guards willing to talk, he located only one man after the war who had come home from the unit Pali was part of. But this man could not help him. The second one he spoke with was a decent person, who was not in Pali's company but in another one in the general area. He returned to Hungary in the spring of 1943 and told my father about the generally practiced, unprecedented cruelties to which the unfortunate servicemen were subjected in the Hungarian army. Withholding food from them, forcing slave laborers to shovel the iced-over soil, making them do hard physical work in mud and snow and rain, the guards compelled the Jewish servicemen to work till they collapsed, many of them dying alongside the road. And if they did not die of exhaustion, hunger, or disease, they froze to death because they had nothing but rags on their backs in the Russian winter, where temperatures dropped to -40°F. He also told my father about the constant brutalities the servicemen had to endure. Among those he recounted was the "entertainment" the guards and officers enjoyed most: they forced the servicemen to perform somersaults for hours or climb high up into the trees in the ice-covered forests, and upon reaching the highest branch, to "crow like roosters." Hearing this account, my poor father fainted.

By the time I arrived home from school that day, my mother told me he was asleep. She also told me what he had heard from the former guard. After this experience, my father sobbed each time we talked about Pali, so that we learned not to mention him in our discussions. I also started to wake up every night, watching the strip of light that would appear under the door separating my room from the library where my father slept. His lights were on as he read in bed. One day I noticed that no matter when I went to bed, the lights in his room were always on. It took some time before I understood that he could not fall asleep at all. I started to keep myself up at night, reading in bed, using a flashlight under my blanket. I did this because I wanted to wait and see when he fell asleep. But I could not wait long enough for darkness to cover the door. I started to wake up at night at different times. To no avail. The lights were always on. Once, I was sick and could not sleep at all. Watching the threshold, I understood that no matter what I did, the golden stripe would never fade. After Pali's draft and disappearance, my father slept for only short stretches during the night till the end of his life. He simply dozed off or daydreamed for just a few periods of time.

And despite the fact that none of the guards with whom he talked could say anything about Pali's possible survival, and despite the fact that after the war he read every book and every eyewitness account about the murder of the Jewish servicemen, he still hoped for Pali's miraculous return. As a result, he kept on searching as long as he lived for people who might have seen his brother, or whose paths might have crossed Pali's. In fact, it was in the early 1960s, twenty years after Pali's "disappearance," as my mother told me after my father's death, that he went to a village to meet with a former guard, not of Pali but of other servicemen, seeking information, but he came away with no particular news. (Then, in the mid-1960s, Iván met with someone claiming to have known Pali. This man asserted that Pali lived to see liberation, but that he was shot by the Russians after they caught him in the company of some of his starving comrades, breaking into a grocery store. The prisoners were stealing sugar . . .)

Even today, periodically, I leave the lights on at night, where I live in Dallas, Texas, thinking for a breathtaking moment that he might have gotten to America, found our address, and is now on his way to visit us. If this were the case, he must see that we are at home, waiting for him.

Margit and her children remained in Békés; my father helped them as much as he could, even later in the worst time under the Communist rule in Hungary, even when we barely had anything to eat. But Pali's tragedy changed our lives, and it changed that of Erzsi too.

"It is terrible," she told me shortly before the German occupation, "that nobody helped him!" And then she thought for a short while: "I believe, had I been in Békés, I could have saved Pali."

"Yes?" I asked, "And how?"

"I don't know," she said. "Perhaps I would have taken him along and hidden him somewhere!"

9

BEFORE THE STORM

I no longer remember when I thought of committing suicide for the first time; I only remember thinking about it more and more. And I know that this thought came quite naturally to me. During those years, we had known a whole family who had committed suicide, and my parents had several friends and acquaintances who had done so as well. In fact, the act of suicide became part of the world in which we lived. This was an act, as I learned much later, that had not been unfamiliar to Hungarians in desperate conditions, nor had it been unfamiliar to Hungarian Jews. Indeed, as historians and cultural critics have often observed, ever since the double suicide of the crown prince of the monarchy, Rudolf, and his lover, Marie Vetsera, at the end of the nineteenth century, a disproportionately large number of Hungarians had committed suicide, including the country's greatest twentieth-century poet, Attila József, in 1937, and its prime minister, Pál Teleki, in 1941. My father, too, had two friends who died of self-inflicted wounds, and, as already mentioned, he had an older brother who killed himself. While at that time I had no knowledge of this whatsoever, there was a general message regarding suicide, which was held up as a means for escaping suffering—or, in Teleki's case, as a means of restoring dignity. I remembered that Hanna spoke of it as well. She wished, she said, she had committed suicide rather than go on living without her father. Looking at my father's face and remembering her statement, I agreed. I knew I did not want to live without him. In fact, when I thought of Pali, imagining him as he dragged himself along in freezing weather on the highways of the Ukraine, only to be shot into a ditch, or as he was sent naked by his torturers to climb up a tree and crow like a rooster, I thought it would have been better had he committed suicide rather than suffer so much; better to have died than become "garbage" at the end anyway. Considering these ideas and images, I thought I preferred to die. While my parents, with whom I talked about this, were outraged on hearing my statements, I thought I could understand those who say no to further anguish. When I said so, however, my parents angrily argued with me, claiming that one never knows whether at the end a bad situation could turn into a good one, and that it is a terrible idea to inflict such pain on the rest of the family. At this point, I stopped the discussion. But I decided that when confronted with separation from them, I would do just that. I had thought about this decision for a long time and felt both comfortable and uneasy about it; comfortable because it promised to save me from living without my parents, and uneasy because it raised unbearably difficult questions. In the case that my father was not killed, how could I cause him such pain? How could I leave him alone? Or would he perhaps want to die with me and leave everyone else behind? Would my mother want to die with us? And Iván? The problem was difficult; and I did not know how to resolve it. "Perhaps," I thought, "all of us should commit suicide." But how?

I could not talk about this dilemma, of course, with anybody. But when I went to sleep at night, I often pondered the questions: When is the moment to go? And how would I do that? What is it I could suggest to my parents? I was afraid of guns; and, of course, I knew nobody who had one. Nor could I imagine myself jumping out of the window of a high-rise, as, I had heard, some of my father's friends had done. On the other hand, I could imagine turning on the gas stove—although, as I heard, gas might cause an explosion. What I decided to do at the end, however, was to find out from my parents where they kept the cyanide my father had brought home from the pharmacy when we left Békéscsaba. I knew they had it: either I overheard them speaking about it to one another, or I overheard some discussion they had with others.

While I do not precisely remember what they said, I understood that we had poison, which, if taken, would end a person's life in a minute or two. Why did my parents bring that poison home? Perhaps because they, too, were contemplating suicide? I will never know. At any rate, I decided I would talk with them about this possibility, telling them my thoughts, proposing that all of us die together. I felt better now; I feared the threat of separation no more. But then, I do not know how and why, I forgot about my plan for months.

As we know today, by 1943 most European Jews had already been killed in the camps or by mass shootings. But in Hungary, the war against the Jews had not yet emerged full scale. In fact, the Hungarian Jews did not even know about Auschwitz. Observing the semi-Fascist Horthy government's attempts at offering even more subservient declarations of loyalty to Germany and an even more subservient involvement with the Reich, most Hungarian Jews saw hope in his behavior. They expected to survive to see the Allies' victory. Every night we listened to the news from the BBC and followed the state of the war on the globe. Iván and my father, as probably most Jews still alive in the country, found themselves deeply involved in discussions on the state of the armies, their various battles, and their victories. And both of them, as well as other people we knew, were convinced of the Allies' growing success on the front, and admired their determination to defeat the Third Reich and win the war. At the same time, we lived in a strange frame of mind. Preoccupied with the war, worrying for Pali, and aware of the threat to the Jews, my parents tried to carry on with daily life as if everything was normal. My father went to work every day; my mother ran the household. Iván and I went to school, had friends over, and played great games with Erzsi whenever she came. Also, I read many books, novels, dramas, and poems; I practiced the piano several hours a day, always playing for my father the pieces at night I had worked on during the day. And we regularly visited opera performances and concerts, both of which, my father said, had been seriously affected by the anti-Jewish measures. In fact, there were now virtually no Jews in the orchestras and just a very few among the solo performers. We also played a lot of music at home.

But something had changed: my father no longer arranged chamber music nights. "We'll play again," he said, his face turning gray and heartbreakingly sad, "when Pali returns."

Still, when my aunt Lulu moved to Budapest, we did start to play again. We went to see her at least once a week. One of her sons, Bandi, had left Hungary earlier for Switzerland (and later went from there to what was then Palestine), but my other cousin, Gábor, was around. He played the cello, and I often played with him as well as listened to him in house concerts they arranged. These circumstances changed by the winter of 1943–44, when Lulu met a man her own age and married him. The couple moved to Tornalja, where they lived until they were rounded up on June 6 or 7, 1944.

But during 1943, no new attacks took place against Hungarian Jews. The deportation of the so-called foreign Jews had been carried out in the summer of 1941, the execution of Jewish men, women, and children by shooting them into the Duna and Tisza rivers in the "Southern Region," in January–February 1942. Certainly the torture and murder of the unfortunate labor servicemen, first on the Eastern front, in Bor, Serbia, and later in Hungary and elsewhere, had not stopped before 1945. But the year 1943 brought no new bloodshed to the Hungarian Jewish community. Of course, as before, Jews were considered second-class citizens. They lived under the pressure of the systematically planned anti-Jewish measures, with a constant threat against their lives, and with the fear and humiliation created by the country's anti-Semitic campaigns in politics and the media. Also, by 1943 most Jews had lost their jobs and businesses, so that they became impoverished. In this respect, too, we were lucky. Financially, our family had done very well. My father had an excellent income. Working fourteen to fifteen hours a day in the bicycle shop, he was enormously grateful for his success. He earned now much more than he had as a pharmacist in Békéscsaba. We lived in a very nice apartment in a house situated in a beautiful neighborhood in Budapest. With the antique furniture my mother had been given by her father and the books my father collected throughout the years, we were surrounded by great beauty and great culture. Although, my father told me, he would not want to sell bicycles after the war, he was happy for the moment to earn so much that we could afford a perfectly satisfying lifestyle. Yet he reminded us again and again that nowadays most Jews were jobless, struggling desperately for their daily existence. And he did everything he could for other people. He supported almost fully Pali's family and gave significant donations to agencies concerned with the upkeep of the new Jewish refugees in Hungary from German-occupied territories.

Despite our financial comfort and awareness of the relative security Hungarian Jews enjoyed in comparison with Jews of most European countries, our parents' sense of danger never faded. Pali's fate was a reminder all the time of the precarious state of our lives, of the danger and threat hovering over all of us. Every new set of refugees escaping to Hungary from the neighboring countries, as well as from Western Europe, hiding from or just bribing the watchdogs of the Hungarian Foreign Office, brought along new horror stories, which revealed quite clearly that we had every reason to live in constant fear and that the probability of a direct attack on our lives was high.

In fact, by 1943, I witnessed more and more discussions on the inevitability of such an attack. Often I fell asleep on our living-room couch while friends of my parents were talking about the atrocities they had direct knowledge of and the hatred and sadism of the Germans they had experienced or fled from. I heard their voices in my dreams. There was no place to escape from them. After a while, even in school or when I practiced, I saw before my eyes German uniforms marching on the streets in Klagenfurt, driving the Jews from their houses, stripping them of their clothes, hosing them down in freezing weather until they froze over, as Jana, our parents' friend who came from Klagenfurt, recounted. And resounding in my head, I heard their orders at the Polish marketplace:

"Men, sixteen to fifty, to the right; women, eighteen to forty-five, to the left; everybody else to the back."

Imagining constantly that they would separate me from my parents, I continued to be consumed by fear. I saw people being tortured, and my father was among them. I saw him from afar; he was standing on a scaffold. I saw him burned, beaten, and stabbed. And I saw myself, alone, running through the streets among burning houses. I did not even need to close my eyes. I saw these images during the day as well as at night. I tried to fight against them, but I did not know how. I could not talk about this terror with anybody because my mother started to cry as soon as I told her how frightened I was. And my father, while holding me in his arms and whispering sweet words about the future into my ears, unwittingly revealed with his face and his bearing that he really did not believe in what he said. In fact, sometimes he could hardly hide his own vision of doom. So time passed, but my fears did not leave me. I tried to fight against them, but I could not. Nor could I talk with anybody about them. Even Iván was annoyed with me, screaming at me that I was acting like a baby. And Erzsi was bothered as well. She did not know what to say; she went back to my parents, crying and hoping they would help me.

The year 1943 came to an end. We sat around in the library room on New Year's Eve, and laughed a lot about certain people who take themselves too seriously. We also ate doughnuts at midnight, and I drank a bit of champagne. But what we enjoyed most was the good news we heard on the BBC. Looking again at the globe and individual maps, and understanding that the war would have to end soon, I believed my father when he said that after the Allies won the war the world would become good again. He said that intelligence and enlightened thinking would overcome madness, and that in the world of the future, we would never again be looked upon with contempt or hatred. I believed him.

It was one in the morning when we went to bed. I hugged and kissed my parents: on that night, I felt happy and secure. On that night, we also left the lights on in the living room as well, even after we went to sleep. In case Pali returned, he would know from afar that we were at home, waiting for him. But he did not come.

10

DISASTER STRIKES
MARCH 19

On February 12, 1944, my father and I went to a concert by Walter Gieseking, the world-renowned German pianist. He played beautifully. But we felt strange and intimidated in the Vigadó, the big concert hall in Budapest, which was crowded with German officers. We stayed till the end. But I could see that my father was enormously concerned.

"I didn't know that there were so many German officers in Budapest," he said in amazement. "How come? Why? What happened?"

A few weeks went by. On Thursday, March 16, Lulu arrived, staying downtown in the Astoria Hotel. All of us were together with her on Friday. On Sunday, March 19, she and my father met at the Gerbeaud, at the time the most wonderful red-brick and marble pastry shop in Budapest. After some cake and coffee there, they wanted to take a leisurely walk back to the hotel. My father intended to help her pick up her suitcase and then accompany Lulu with her son Gábor to the train station. As my father explained later, he and Lulu were engaged in an intense discussion, strolling toward the Astoria, when they noticed an unusual commotion in the street. Watching it for a while, they saw a group of German officers in front of the hotel; some of them went inside; others came outside through the glass door. In the street people were hurrying along, looking neither to the right nor to the left, just staring straight ahead. Then they noticed that the traffic had changed: it slowed down significantly. My father was ill at ease; his apprehension intensified. He went inside the hotel with Lulu and Gábor. Her suitcase was already in the lobby; she had put it there before they left. Then the place had been empty; now, groups of German officers were moving about, waiting, talking, explaining things to one another, and laughing. My father told me after the war that at this point, he had been frozen over, his heart beating in his throat.

Lulu stood in line at the cash register; there were others leaving as well. In fact, more people were paying now and going away than usual. After waiting for a while, she paid, and the three of them left. On the way to the station, they had seen Germans in cars, Germans in buses, Germans in trucks. By now, all of them suspected the worst. My father accompanied Lulu and Gábor to the train station and then hurried home.

He did not yet know that the German armed forces had invaded Hungary, nor that the German officers establishing their headquarters at the Astoria Hotel were members of the Gestapo, entering Budapest that morning under the command of Hans Geschke. Their task was the implementation of the Final Solution.

11

PLANS FOR THE FUTURE

On the same Sunday morning, I got up early. But I did not go with my father to meet Lulu; I was preparing for an 11:00 A.M. piano lesson with Mr. Faragó. I wanted to practice a few hours before I had to leave. Planning to study five Chopin mazurkas with him that morning, I hoped to play excellently because I had been invited to perform them at a recital on March 26. I practiced many hours every day, learned these pieces well, and was willing to work much harder to achieve the best results. I was looking forward to this lesson enormously. I hoped for his involvement, going through the mazurkas in great detail, and for his teaching me how to play them ever more beautifully. I wanted to learn from him how I could do my best and become a wonderful pianist. I adored him. In fact, despite my twelve years, I was in love with him and deeply wished that he could see in me a great and beautiful woman and a potentially momentous artist, ready for his inspiration.

I left home at ten minutes before 11:00 A.M.. He lived near us, on Alpár Street. Hurrying across Abonyi Street and then crossing Aréna Street, I noticed how quiet everything was. I saw an empty streetcar and three near-empty buses from afar on Thököly Street, and very few people anywhere. I remember thinking this emptiness unusual. Running up the stairs, I arrived at Mr. Faragó's apartment. As always, his mother opened the door. She was crying. That was strange. I entered. He had just finished a telephone conversation. Looking at me, flabbergasted, he said,

"For heaven's sake! You shouldn't be here!"

"I thought I had a lesson at eleven," I answered slowly, terribly disappointed by this reception.

"This morning the Germans have occupied Hungary! Your parents don't know that?"

"No," I said quietly. The Chopin mazurkas took wing and left me behind. Panic overcame me. Sharply and clearly, the image of Hanna's marketplace emerged before my eyes.

"I cannot let you go home alone." He held my arm. "I'll take you back."

I was silent during the walk, and so was he, saying just a few words.

"Bad times are coming," he said, his voice tense, his eyes teary. "I can only hope that I'll be able to help you and others."

My heart tightened. "He and Erzsi," I thought, "they would risk their lives for us!" But I also wondered about *how* he would be able to do that. I knew from my father that Faragó was born as a Christian to a Christian mother; but he had a Jewish father, who had left the family when the children were infants. Perhaps because his father had never been around, Faragó was not registered as a Jew. Still, his "mixed" origins were not forgotten by the country's watchdogs of racial purity. He had lost his job as a professor at the Franz Liszt Music Academy back in 1941, shortly after the third anti-Jewish law was promulgated. Clearly the racial laws formulated in Nürnberg in 1935 and decreed in Hungary in 1941 would not permit his Jewish ancestry to be overlooked. Yet while the anti-Semitic cultural leadership had tried to kick him out of the academy as early as 1939, Ernő Dohnányi, the world-famous Hungarian pianist, composer, and director of the Music Academy, stopped that action. But by 1941, the anti-Semitic movement had poisoned the country's political and cultural climate to such a degree that Faragó had to be fired as a racially undesirable person. While I did not understand everything as clearly during our walk on that Sunday morning as I did later, I certainly grasped that he was a hero who would sacrifice himself for his friends' sake. And I was right, he did.

He was not talkative during our short stroll. But he walked next to me, and I felt safe. What I could not know at this point of my life was that

I would never again have piano lessons with him. Although we met many times during the spring, summer, and fall of 1944, there were no occasions for lessons anymore. But when I saw him with my father in April 1944, waiting for him to come to his music room, we suddenly noticed two children in the chamber next to ours: the older, a girl, was his student, a pianist, and her little brother, both of whom he hid, along with their mother, for several weeks during the spring of 1944, as I heard their story after the war. Also, he visited us a few times during the summer of that year, even though the house we lived in on Abonyi Street was designated a "Yellow-Star House" and had been marked by a huge yellow Star of David ever since June 17. For "Christians" to visit such houses was by itself dangerous, unless the visitor, if questioned, could produce a reasonable excuse for his presence. Each time Faragó came to us, he gave the caretaker of our apartment house both money and elaborate reasons for his visit. He was then allowed to enter. During these visits, again and again, Faragó offered us his help. My father, whose close friend he had become over the years, was immensely touched by his behavior, for such courage was by no means typical during the spring and summer of 1944. As a matter of fact, one after the other, our acquaintances and friends either completely withdrew; or worse, if my father asked them, they flatly refused to help.

Still, as my father later told me, he was hesitant to accept Faragó's offer for us to move into his apartment after the family that hid there had made a special arrangement with the Germans and left the country. He feared that the young man was being watched, and if we went to live with him, we would soon be discovered, bringing disaster on them as well as on ourselves. Then Faragó fell ill during the early part of the summer; his doctors believed he had a stomach ulcer (only later did they discover that he had pancreatic cancer). By July–August 1944, he had recovered some and visited us frequently in the ghetto house, bringing me chocolate as well as the scores of Mozart and Beethoven sonatas, offering again and again his help to my parents.

But we could not, of course, foresee all this when we parted on March 19, in front of our apartment house on Abonyi Street. We said farewell to one another, and I cried because I feared they would soon march us to the marketplace, as Hanna had described the German occupation to me, and I would never see him again. Indeed, all I saw before my eyes was the dark, garbage-covered, blood-stained marketplace, where Hanna had lost her father and grandfather, and where, I feared, we would soon be taken and murdered. I went up the stairs and rang our doorbell, noting immediately that neither my mother, enthusiastically cooking in the kitchen, nor Iván, getting ready to meet with his friends, knew what had happened.

"Do not go anywhere," I warned him. "The Germans have occupied Hungary."

My mother leaned against the wall, her face turning pale. Iván laughed.

"Come on," he said. "I was just listening to the radio. They are playing Beethoven. If anything suspicious were around, we would be told."

"No! Please, don't go anywhere," I said. "Faragó brought me home. He told me that terrible things might happen on the streets!"

"I don't believe in rumors," he said contemptuously, shaking his finger at me, his silly little sister. He was ready to go out. But as he opened the door to leave, my father entered. Looking at his face, we did not need to say or ask a thing.

He told us in a sentence about Lulu's departure; and going inside the apartment, he pressed me and Iván to his heart with such anguish that I knew I was right when I felt that the world had come to an end. Again my mother started to cry. Iván was silent; and I started to brace myself to be strong, to be able to say what I had decided to propose to my parents in case we were threatened by separation, torture, or death. First, however, my father went to the bookshelves, looking for papers that he had prepared some time ago, explaining to us where to find money and valuables if we needed instantaneous resources, or where to look for help in case he was taken away. Speaking of several things at once, he also was thinking aloud about the ways in which the three of us perhaps could be saved.

"And you," I screamed. "What about you?"

"Well," he said, "it would make no sense now to concentrate on me. First of all, I am a man who will probably be drafted. That means they will look for me everywhere. Although I am forty-six, it doesn't mean that they will shy away from throwing me into the labor service. And if so, I will try to survive. I am pretty strong; probably nothing will happen to me! Second, children can always disappear more easily than adults. And so can, I think, those women who have no workplace."

"I'm not going anywhere without you," I sobbed, evoking every word, every image of Hanna. But he was unbending. Convinced that the Germans would first want to see the "de-Jewification of the capital," and only later that of the countryside, as had been the case in Austria (and as, we learned later, Eichmann wanted to carry out in Hungary), he believed we should flee Budapest. As a matter of fact, he feared that the removal of the Jews and mass deportations would start right here, right now. He was wrong, but he could not know it yet. For the moment, he tried to think of ways for us to escape.

"It would be best if the three of you left Budapest immediately," he said. Then he stopped. "But where to?" he pondered. "Right now, none of us has false papers . . . That doesn't mean, of course, I couldn't get you some tomorrow. But then, the fact that Iván is Jewish would still be easy to ascertain, *unfortunately!* They just have to pull down his pants. That Zsuzsi and Mother are Jewish could not be hidden for long either. Unfortunately," and he covered his face with his hands, "at this point, there is no other place to go, but to Pali's wife, Margit, in Békés. She would, of course, have to hide you because the neighbors might immediately recognize and denounce you. Still, Margit would do this for us anyway."

But he could not call her right away; she did not have a telephone.

At this moment, I went berserk. This was the nightmare I had foreseen in years past; this was the nightmare that had weighed down on me for years; this was the nightmare I was prepared to fight against.

"I am not going away from you," I screamed. "I don't want to see you lying bloody in a ditch! No, no, no! I don't want to live alone and in constant fear that one day they will find me."

I suddenly relived Hanna's story, finally voicing the thoughts I had had over the years: "Please, let's commit suicide together! If we do that, we won't ever be separated. If not, we will be. Let's avoid it! I know that you have cyanide."

The secret was out in the open. They finally understood that I knew they might have considered it.

And then I added, "I know that you don't want to hear this, but taking it, we would die within a few seconds—this is what mother told Anni during a discussion they had about the Germans. Please, let's not suffer; let's not be separated as Hanna was from her father; let's die together!"

After several years of thinking about the threat of separation, I could finally say what I felt.

With wide eyes, my mother looked at me. "I had to live for forty-six years to hear my twelve-year-old say this," she sighed bitterly. But then, she broke down and cried, "Perhaps she is right, perhaps she is right, perhaps she is right."

Was there relief in my father's eyes? Or was it just my imagination?

"Dum spiro, spero" [As long as I live, I hope], he replied very slowly, quoting Latin, as he always did. But then he added, "Now, however, new times are coming . . ."

The conversation stopped for a second.

"They will separate us and put us into gas chambers," I said, and shivered. "I will be alone; and I don't want to suffer."

How did I know about gas chambers on March 19, 1944? I cannot answer the question, for knowledge regarding the extermination camps, including gassing, had not yet spread to Hungary. As we know today, Rudolf Vrba and Alfréd Wetzler had not yet left Auschwitz, so I could not have heard anything about their mission. Thinking hard again and again about this question ever since I have understood its particular significance, I have come to the conclusion that I probably had over-heard something about the gassing vans from one of our guests visiting my parents. These vans were used by the Germans, first in Poland and Serbia, and by 1942 in Russia. I could have been asleep on the couch of our living room when I heard these words uttered; or I could have listened in on discussions between my father and someone from the front or a refugee whom we had met on the street. I know that my parents had many friends and acquaintances; among them were former soldiers, labor servicemen, refugees, Jewish federation officials, business people with connections to the military and the Ministry of the Interior. Did I overhear some discussions on the street or at home while I was half-asleep? I do not remember. But I know that in the early part of the after-noon on March 19, 1944, I spoke of "gas chambers," and that while I did so, I saw, as I had seen in my nightmares for some time by then, a small room and a gas stove turned on, with gas whistling from the burners. I had already breathed in my dreams the sweet, vanilla-scented, smother-ing smell, which attacked my senses and choked my breath. I did not want to die in it: I did not want to suffocate; nor did I want to be left alone and forced to confront it somewhere.

In horror, my parents listened. They did not seem to be enormously surprised by what I said. Nor did they have the strength to argue against me: they just listened. Iván looked at them, then at me. Then he jumped up. "Say whatever nonsense you want to say," he said angrily, even his ears turning red. "And stick your thumbs up your asses," he added. "I am certainly not going to die with you! I want to go on and live! And, perhaps, all of us will!"

"We won't, Iván, we won't," I cried. "They will separate us and kill us at the end!"

"And if they don't? You may do whatever you want, but without me." He left the room and banged the door. Then, suddenly, his head appeared in the door frame: "But sticking your thumb up your asses is the best way of committing suicide."

My parents stared; they even smiled faintly.

Responding to Iván or to something else, who knows what, we did not commit suicide on March 19; and this scene of wild despair and naked horror of wanting to do so never recurred, not even when the Nyilas took my father away on October 20, 1944. I did not bring it up ever again, not even when we were living in hiding, not even when I was alone, separated from everyone, and bombs and shells smashed the windows and the furniture in the room where I was, not even when I was running for cover but did not find it.

Nor did the discussion about leaving Budapest ever come up again. That was our luck. We soon found out that had we tried to go to the train station on the afternoon of March 19, we would likely have been stopped by either German or Hungarian military units that were asking people for identification papers at every major train station in Hungary on that day (except during the noon hour when Lulu had left), arresting and interning all the Jews entering the terminal. In fact, nearly a thousand Jews were stopped and arrested that day. All of them were marched to the camp at Kistarcsa, kept there for several months, and then, with the rest of the prisoners, deported to Auschwitz-Birkenau. Lulu was lucky to avoid this fate and live a few months longer. But most people who went to the train stations that Sunday were not so fortunate—among them my friend and teacher, the poet Magdi Soós, who wanted to look up the train schedule for the next day to visit her relatives. Instead, she was arrested and "transferred" to Auschwitz. She survived and returned to Budapest in the summer of 1945.

Just like the discussion of suicide on the afternoon of March 19, 1944, my father's suggestion that we go to and hide in Békés was no longer considered by anybody in our family: it ceased to be an option for us. But the threat of immediate disaster could not be covered up anymore. I lived with death fears, trembling for the life of my father and mother, of Iván and Erzsi. Yet for some reason or other, I gave up the idea of suicide altogether.

12

MEASURES TAKEN

The rest of the afternoon of March 19 passed as if in a haze. Erzsi arrived in the evening. She had just heard what had happened from her Russian friend Marina, who had fled from the Reds with her parents in 1917 and lived now with her mother in Buda, in the same apartment house as Erzsi. They wanted to go to the movies, but when Erzsi arrived at Marina's apartment, she was confronted with the news of the occupation. In fact, Marina told her that she had decided to marry her German boyfriend as quickly as possible because, otherwise, as a Russian refugee, she might suffer terribly. Confused and frightened, Erzsi could think of nothing other than coming to see us. She rang the bell. I opened the door. Her hands were trembling, and she was crying. The only sentence she could utter was framed as a declaration: "I will never leave you!"

Stepping into the entrance hall, she told my parents she would do everything to save our family. And if she could not do so, she sobbed, she would come with us wherever we were taken. My father agreed that for the night, she could stay in our apartment, but he insisted she find a place to move to tomorrow because, in the long run, she would not be able to stay with us. In fact, he convinced her to rent a room nearby that might, in case of an emergency, help her and us a great deal. She did so the next day. Moving in, she came back to us and helped my mother all day. Telling the caretaker that she was moving her own things from our apartment, she packed parcel after parcel, containing bedclothes, blankets, warm coats, and pullovers, carrying them one after the other out of the house. Hurrying to the post office, she mailed them to Békéscsaba, to her parents. My mother and father hoped that, in this way, some of our warm clothing could be saved. They could not foresee, however, that less than a year later, after the siege and occupation of Budapest by the Soviet forces, we would flee from the capital to Békéscsaba. Emaciated, freezing, with our clothes torn and worn down, we then found our warm coats, pullovers, and blankets waiting for us in the house of Erzsi's parents. And we found not only our winter clothes! Erzsi sent home some of my dolls, board games, even my favorite books, so that I could read and play with the neighbors' children after the war. Hence, we not only had clean and warm clothing during the day and warm bedding at night, but I found also a connection to my previous life with my old toys and games.

Having mailed the packages, Erzsi started to visit her friends and relatives. She even went out of town to places where people she knew lived, trying to convince them of the need to help us or help her identify others who could do so. She also went to various addresses my father gave her and tried to make lists of everyone she could visit. My father, too, left the house every day between 11:00 A.M. and 1:00 P.M., the time period allotted to the Jews for the purchase of food. During these hours, he too tried to meet and visit with friends and find contacts with people who, he hoped, would help us. He wanted to work out a plan for us to hide somewhere and avoid the roundups that were, he believed, inevitably coming. In this way, he thought, we could escape the concentration and entrainment of the Jewish community of Budapest. He visited old friends, colleagues, and acquaintances, begging them for help. But for the moment, he did not have much success. Coming home more tired every day, he did not have anything to tell us. I saw on his face that he was not being successful. In fact, I could clearly see despair and anguish changing his looks and bearing.

He just wanted to find somebody to rely on, he told me. Of course, he already knew two people on earth on whom he could rely: Erzsi and Gyuri Faragó. And he was, of course, enormously grateful for their dedication to us. Yet he still felt helpless. He did not quite see how, in the long run, either of them could offer us the kind of help he thought we needed: hiding us before the rounding up and deportation of the Jewish community. At the beginning of June, Faragó again offered us his apartment to hide in. But, as already mentioned, he was half-Jewish and known as such by many, including his enemies. Hence, he lived under the watchful eyes of his neighbors: the entrance door of his apartment opened from the corridor above a courtyard. Whoever visited him could be watched by his neighbors; whoever left his apartment could be seen not only by people living next to him but also by those living under or above his dwelling. Obviously my father's fears were justified: despite Gyuri's heroic sacrifice, we could not feel secure in his apartment. In fact, we could be easily spotted there by his neighbors and denounced to the police.

As for Erzsi, I think, at first, my father did not look upon her as an independent, powerful human being, as an adult, who had the means and rank in society to physically or psychologically resist and wage a war against the Germans, or the Hungarian gendarmeries, or the police. She did not own a house or an apartment where we could have moved; she did not have a job or a business she could have relied on; she was not a member of any established community that would look upon her as a contributing member. She was a young girl, obviously lacking the power to care for and shelter our family twenty-four hours a day. What my father had not yet discovered was Erzsi's enormous inner strength, endurance, and love for us, her courage in defying all obstacles, and her capacity for resisting menace and life-threatening danger. He considered Erzsi the world's best playmate for me, a sweetheart, a loving child, whom he could trust and use for his various plans invented to save our lives. But that Erzsi would be able to change the world of destruction and death into the realm of goodness, love, and self-sacrifice, my father did not know, and could not even imagine in the spring of 1944.

Despite the fears he lived with, he never spoke to us of the darkness he now saw enveloping the world. We just noticed that while despair started to possess him more and more, he tried to act as if he believed that everything would fall into place before destruction would take over, emphasizing and demonstrating that he was essentially an optimist. Of course, at times, he indeed was. Discussing with us the war in detail, and thinking about the fronts a great deal, he described the Germans' defeat as imminent. He explored the difficulties the Reich now faced everywhere and tried to draw conclusions for the future. He explained again and again that the war would soon end, and, obviously fighting against his own fears, he started to insist on the "reality" of his observation, attempting to convince himself of the fact that the Germans had no more time left for taking us out of the country.

"Our liberation is in the hands of the Allies," he told me, his face burning with excitement, "and we must recognize that the end of the war and the defeat of Germany are imminent."

I would have loved to believe him. But with the German occupation of Hungary, my fear of the future made me tremble constantly. Watching him, I did not quite believe in his optimistic vision of the world, at least in the vision he tried to pass on to me. For what he repeated over and over involved the argument that the Germans would no longer have either the time or the means to take us out of the country. Poor father. He did not yet know, as no one could even have imagined, that it would take less than two months, from May 15 to July 7, 1944, for the Hungarian gendarmerie to deport the entirety of Hungarian Jewry in the countryside, some 437,000 people, most of them to Auschwitz-Birkenau. Of course, those in Budapest did not yet know and could not even imagine the goal, the extent, or the purpose of the deportations. Therefore, sometimes some of them still believed in and hoped for miracles. Small wonder that when in June and July of 1944 the news of mass deportations all over the country finally reached the Jews of Budapest, my father tried to tell us that *after* the invasion of the Allies in Normandy, such a huge undertaking would be improbable, in fact, impossible to carry out *in* the capital of Hungary.

I remember more or less every day of the spring and summer of 1944: we read and were witness to the promulgation of the new anti-Jewish decrees that appeared almost daily in the newspapers. We read the measure providing for the removal of books by Jews or by Christians of Jewish ancestry from every public library and every school library in the country. We saw the decree enacting the requisition for housing, and knew that groups were being set up by the government to throw Jews out of their apartments. We read the decrees prohibiting the employment of Jews and the dismissal of Jewish civil servants and lawyers, actors, and journalists from the professional chambers. We even knew about the law demanding that Jews declare their motor vehicle ownership. And then, we read the most hair-raising law of all: the law demanding that Jews wear a 3.8 x 3.8–inch, six-pointed, canary-yellow Star of David, made of cloth and sewn on the left chest of the clothing of every Jewish man, woman, and child under the sun.

It all started to become reality. We had to dismiss our wonderful cleaning lady, Éva, who had worked in our house for many years. Iván had to turn in his motorcycle, which he loved so much. And my mother started to sew badges on our clothing so that we could appear in public after April 5, 1944, the day we had to start wearing the yellow star. This day was also Iván's fifteenth birthday. Waking up early in the morning, we went to the window and watched the street, waiting for people walking under the window with the yellow star fixed on their clothing. Staring at the pavement, we finally saw someone. He wore a dark coat; fixed on it and gleaming was the yellow star. He looked grotesque, walking cautiously, looking around right and left. Later my father went out, and then Iván, each with the glaring yellow star fastened on their jackets. A few days later, I had to leave the house accompanied by my mother, hurrying to the dentist. I was waiting for thunder and lightning, for an earthquake, or a voice to speak out from above or from the deep. But in fact, nothing happened. And I do not even know the reaction of other people who saw me because I could not look up. I could not look into anybody's eyes. I simply watched the movement of my shoes.

But I could see that my father was very upset. I overheard my mother and Erzsi discussing that he had failed to line up friends, colleagues, and acquaintances who would be willing to help, or who would be able to locate others to hide us somewhere. Nor had he yet found anyone who would sell him false papers, or who would help us to flee from the country. But after a couple of months, going from district to district, from person to person, following every indication and suggestion, looking at place after place, sometimes alone, sometimes with Erzsi, he, as I overheard the whispers between him and my mother, had succeeded in finding connections to the black market, so that he could buy false passports and whatever else he thought we needed. He roamed the streets to visit people; he even took streetcars or buses during the hours when Jews were allowed to appear in public. We did not know it then—only in the course of the next few weeks did the news reach us—that the police in the city and the gendarmerie in the suburbs were periodically stopping the streetcars, buses, and the metro, picking up Jews, who were easily recognizable with (or without) the yellow star. At times they also blocked a few arbitrarily chosen streets in Budapest, stopping the passersby, asking for identification papers. The Jews caught in this way were taken to jail, or worse, sent to Kistarcsa, the internment camp near Budapest. Kept there for a while, these Jews, like those arrested during the first few days of the occupation, were entrained and deported to Auschwitz. But we did not know about this in March and April 1944. Hence my father continued his daily trips for help. And we were enormously lucky: he never was caught, never was arrested. In fact, after a while, his search reached a kind of completion: he found not only false papers for us but also contact with two or three priests in the Catholic Church. The newest rumors had it that those who converted would not be taken out of the country, so, on a warm June day, he and my mother went to a mass conversion. They became Catholic. Iván and I were also to be converted, but somehow the rumor turned out to be untrue, so we remained unchristened for the time being.

The rest of the family stayed at home all the time. Erzsi shopped for us. She went "home" to her rented room every night, though, so that her landlady would see her daily and would not have to wonder where she was. Also, she spent time with her relatives and friends living in Budapest, and she went to places on our behalf in the countryside where my father could not go. But she was with us most of the time, especially during the first few weeks of the occupation. She helped my mother in the kitchen and continued to play fantasy games and make-believe with me, driven by an intensity that helped me, and, I think, helped her to live with the danger threatening our lives.

13

THE NEW WORLD

I remember, it was after the first few weeks of the German occupation that I noticed something strange: people around me, including our friends, acquaintances, even members of my own family, stopped speaking about (perhaps even ceased to consider) the threat we were facing. In fact, recalling my observations during those few weeks, I remember that I noticed people's *desire* to forget about the danger. Almost all the adults I knew seemed to discuss nothing else but their concern for the long-term availability of tea and coffee supplies or their involvement in games of bridge and chess. It is possible, of course, that they simply did not know how to react in this state of entrapment by deadly danger, but they appeared to be shocked into silence during the first two or three weeks of the occupation. I remember, even my father seemed to be paralyzed. I, on the other hand, could think of nothing else but the atrocities I had heard about for years. In fact, all I saw before my eyes was Hanna's marketplace, with corpses dripping with blood piled on top of one another. Yet nobody wanted to talk with me about this. I trembled when I thought that we might be separated from one another and shot into different piles. When I turned to my mother, she became distraught, her tear-ravaged face even more anguished, as soon as I started to talk about Hanna. She simply called either Iván or my father, hoping they would distract me. But after a while, she seemed to me more worried about her sewing machine than about the future, complaining about how terrible it would be if she could not sew when we would need her to mend our clothing. Nor was my father talking about the horrors facing us.

He claimed that we would be saved by the Allies' war against Germany. And Iván did not even come when called upon to talk or to play with me; he just wanted to assemble a radio, using the pieces of some old wires and electrical equipment my parents kept in the basement. He wanted to do this because we had had to surrender the radio we owned, and he thought we must have one if we wanted to follow the events of the war.

After a while, even Erzsi, who was at first very frightened of the Germans, acted like a great optimist.

"I am sure," she said, "in fact, I can foretell that we'll see the end of the war, and that we'll live happily ever after."

I was glad to hear this, but I could not help wondering: What would happen if the Germans would not let us do so? And I did not understand any of this. Was my father less afraid now or did he just want to keep the danger away from me? It did not take long for him to stop pretending.

"The Allies have landed in Normandy," screamed Iván on June 6, running out of the apartment, banging the doors and ringing the doorbells of our neighbors, telling them what had happened. In a few minutes our apartment was crowded with people. Looking at the globe on our table, we could follow the events on the eastern and western front alike.

"How long can it last then?" was my first question.

Most of the visitors agreed: "Not for long."

"A few more months, perhaps," said my father when he tucked me in at night.

"But what can happen to us in the next few weeks?" I asked.

"We hope the Germans won't have time for anything other than defending themselves," he said and smiled.

Every morning he left the house, planning to meet with people, searching for friends, trying to find help for us. Driven by a passionate urge to change our lot, he felt, I think, that he could only act, assess, and decide upon the emerging possibilities when he thought through them with people he trusted. This search for ways to defend us against the Germans gave him strength to live from one day to another, even to remain whole till almost the end. Indeed, after a while, his search began to bear fruit. First of all, he came home every day with news, which those staying in their apartments had no opportunity to hear. This fact alone helped to relieve our isolation. But most important, he found some people through friends of friends who promised him their help if deportation orders were issued—even though they would require lots of money and act only under certain circumstances. Still, the very fact that he had located human beings who would help us made him feel much better, relying on their promise, hoping for our liberation.

Swollen half-moons under his eyes, bright yellow star on his gray jacket, his face pale and careworn but determined, he walked back and forth between Abonyi Street and the world outside, in which he hoped to secure a safe house for us. When he smiled, I felt that the world had become a much better place. I watched him every morning from the window as he went outside; and I followed his steps from afar as he strolled home. He was as heartbreakingly handsome as ever! And I loved him so much. Although I did not want him to leave every morning, I knew I could not stop his doing so. Thus he left, and, with enormous luck, he always returned before the hours allotted for the Jews came to an end. And no matter what he saw or what happened on his way, he always brought us something delightful: a paper doll, an apple, even some flowers. Later, when the night came and I went to bed, he came to tuck me in, whispering into my ear:

"Sleep well, darling! You'll see, the Germans will lose the war! We'll be free again, and we'll have a beautiful life! You'll play the piano and concertize, and we'll clap for you until you play eleven encores!"

I curled up under the quilt and did not dare to ask the question torturing me.

Night after night went by; then, suddenly, I could not take it any longer. It was the middle of June, and I heard some terrible rumors about the Germans shooting Jews. I could not hold myself back.

"And what about Pali?" I asked.

"He'll return, perhaps," he said. "I pray for him every night."

But he never spoke about him. Nor did we bring up his name. On the other hand, he spoke of Lulu all the time. He was worried: we did not know anything about her. His last two letters to her came back stamped with large letters: MOVED. But neither she nor we had access to a telephone, which the Jews had had to surrender in mid-April, so we could not call anybody. And in vain had Erzsi and Gyuri Faragó tried to call her number; they were out of luck. For the same reason, we did not have any contact with my aunts, uncles, and cousins in Szabadka either. Forbidden to travel or to call, we lost all means of communication with one another. My mother, too, was worried about her brother and sisters. Then, by the end of June, we heard that the Jews of Szabadka had been moved to the ghetto and transported from there by train. My mother was most worried about Anni. Crippled and sickly, Anni was obviously unable to bear physical hardship.

"I hope they put her into a wheelchair when they moved her somewhere." My mother looked far away, her face teary, pale, and sad. "After all, she can't walk more than five minutes on her crutches."

She certainly could not. Poor Anni. She was crammed and locked into a boxcar without food and water for four days, in the heat of June, with eighty people, as were her brother, Imre, with his thirteen-year-old son (my cousin Gyurika) and the rest of my mother's sisters and their husbands. If she had survived the journey, of which we have no report whatsoever, Anni had been instantaneously sent into one of the gas chambers of Auschwitz-Birkenau. Nor did the Germans prepare a wheelchair for her. She was probably chased on foot from the train to the gas chamber. And if she did not die of the chase, she died of hydrogen cyanide poisoning inside that place, as did most Hungarian Jews. The truth of the matter is that we have never learned the details of Anni's torturous end. None of those who had been with her, including the rest of my mother's siblings, returned. I shudder each time I think of their lives and deaths, including the suffering of this warm-hearted, sweet, superbly intelligent person and her pain and humiliation before her death.

Despite the lack of personal communication during the late spring of 1944, the Jewish community of Budapest was not as isolated from the world as were the Jews of the countryside. It was not locked up in a ghetto; it was not "processed for deportation." We were even aware of the stages of the war: luckily, we had a radio. Indeed, despite the fact that we had been forced to surrender ours, Iván put one together from scratch. The prohibition notwithstanding, we listened to the BBC every night. This was a difficult enterprise, though, because in practice just one person could sit down and listen to the news; the rest of us had to be on guard. We had to be ready to turn off and hide the radio immediately if someone should drive along or even walk toward the house. This meant that each time people listened to the news, others had to watch the streets from all the windows, noting anybody coming close to the house (or even hearing a car, as the Germans rode around the city trying to catch through radio waves those who listened to the BBC). Yet despite the high tension this operation required and the risk we took resisting the order, Iván and my father listened to the news daily. In this way, we were aware of what was happening on the front all the time, which, in turn, provided us with the knowledge that put the daily threat against our lives in perspective and offered us at least some hope for escape and survival.

Also, partly because my father and Erzsi were constantly carrying messages to and from our friends, we always had some exchange with other people. This interaction was possible, of course, because we had not yet been forced out of our homes. That is, the Jews of Budapest were significantly more independent than those in the provinces, who were crammed into ghettos and forced to live under the watching eyes of their neighbors, the gendarmerie, and their hostile guards. The rope was yet to be tightened around our necks, while it was *already* tightened around the necks of the Jews in the countryside. They were first to go. Our poor, poor relatives in Szabadka, Kiskunfélegyháza, Kanizsa, and Tornalja were isolated from everybody and everything. They had no one to rely on, no one to trust, no one to keep up with, no one to take and bring messages back and forth. Throughout the long spring of 1944, nobody could communicate with us from these towns, nor from my birthplace, where my parents had lived for many years; as a matter of fact, nobody recounted or told us about the weeks of anguish, fear, and captivity, nor about the ghettoization and deportation of our relatives.

In the course of the spring of 1944, however, we were hit by a further series of anti-Jewish measures. Not only did the new decrees provide for the closing and confiscation of every Jewish business, including my father's bicycle shop with Louis, but one of them, in late April, also reduced the food supply for Jews. My parents were gasping for air.

"What will happen to us?" they asked. "What to do? Where to hide? Where to go?"

And then, as I overheard them talking to one another: "And the children? Will we die of starvation?"

A bit later, however, my parents took turns listening, even holding fast, to Erzsi's promise, that no matter what, she would bring us food every day. Today I am not sure whether or not, at this point, they realized our powerlessness and just gave up the fight. Or is it possible that under the pressure of the threat of starvation both of them arrived at the end of any rational thought and decided to rely on miracles? Did they just pretend to wait for miracles? Or could it have been that over time they started to feel the impact of Erzsi's relentless confession of love, and started to believe in her power, without asking questions, without trying to solve the puzzle: "If we are locked into the ghetto, how will she be able to visit us?"

Rumors of ghettoization swept through our life in the middle of April, but the process itself did not materialize in Budapest before the middle of June. Not so in the countryside, where the roundup of the Jews and their concentration in tobacco and brick factories and other similar auxiliary detention places started in mid-April, leading directly to the systematic deportation of the Jewish community. This deportation process was carried out between May 15 and July 7, 1944, following a well-defined plan from zone to zone, into which the country had been divided. But at this point, in Budapest, most people did not know what was taking place in the countryside. First of all, communication among Jewish families had been cut off completely. Neither had the BBC, other radio stations, or the community councils given an account of the systematic de-Jewification process carried out in every province of the country. Even my parents came to understand what had really taken place only when they were confronted with the first eyewitness accounts emerging from Békéscsaba. And this happened only by chance, after Mrs. Tevan and Zsuzsi Tevan, our former neighbors and good friends, escaped the entrainment in Békéscsaba and arrived in Budapest. Originally they had lived on Andrássy Street, in the same house where we had lived until 1941, in the house where our former pharmacy had been located.

Arriving in Budapest, Klári Tevan, whose husband, Andor Tevan, had been the director and owner of one of Hungary's most outstanding small presses, sent a message to my father, asking him to come and see her, shortly after she fled with her daughter from Békéscsaba. She was eager to tell my father about their experiences, warning him to hide as soon as he found an acceptable refuge. First of all, she told him about the horrid scenes of torture and murder that played themselves out after the establishment of the ghetto in Békéscsaba, describing the gendarmerie's cruel treatment and the deplorable condition of the area's Jews. Suffering in the ghetto with the rest of the people for a while, the two Tevans eventually escaped entrainment. They fled from the place with the help of both Péter (Pierre) Szabó, a fabulously elegant and sweet middle-aged gentleman, and his courageous French wife, Madeleine. The couple, as Mrs. Tevan recounted, smuggled the Tevans out of the ghetto, helping them to flee from Békéscsaba to Budapest by train. After they succeeded in escaping untold dangers, the Szabós escorted the Tevans to a safe house in the capital. As my father and mother considered Klári's experience and the tale of the tobacco factory in Békéscsaba, where thousands of Jews were forced to move, and where, to extort more gold and money, the gendarmes and the police beat up and tortured a group of intellectuals and businessmen, my parents fully understood the reality of our position. They also understood that there would be no mercy and no escape.

Yet there were still some issues not yet recognized by my parents—as a matter of fact, not even by the Tevans. No one knew what lay in wait *after* the deportation, nor did they know that the treatment of the Jews in Békéscsaba was an integral part of the destruction process of all Jews in Hungary, of all Jews in Europe.

Still, whatever they knew, at this point my father must have lived in tremendous fear. The rumors of the deportation in the countryside started to spread to Budapest. Then, sometime in June, we received a handwritten note from Gábor, my cousin, Lulu's younger son. He was in hiding in Budapest, but he had copied down and sent us the text of Lulu's postcard of June 8, which she had sent him from the Tornalja ghetto. At this time, Gábor was hiding in the house of his aunt Manci (his father's sister), who had married a Christian and lived in Budapest. Lulu's text was carefully written, her words indirect. Using a pseudonym for the sender of the card, she had obviously been afraid that people in the Tornalja post office might identify her name, read the card, become suspicious, and denounce her to the police. Hence, underlying the message she wrote emerged an otherwise invisible text without which the meaning of the words she used could not be understood. On the surface, the text referred to "vacation time," which obviously alluded, like the word "illness," to the impending deportation. Reading the actual text beneath this surface, we understood that Lulu knew the truth: she knew that from the journey on which she would be sent now she would never return.

"My dearest Manci: Probably tomorrow we'll go on a vacation. I am not sure how this trip will affect our health; I am afraid, adversely. Please write to your nephew [Manci's nephew was Gábor, Lulu's son, the young man hiding at Manci's] and look after him. In turn, he should write his stepbrother [the son of her second husband, Dr. Fenyő]. They [she meant the two young men] will perhaps be able to avoid this illness [the impending deportation]. My kisses to parents and children alike. When I meet Bélus [Lulu's first husband, Gábor's father, who had died years before], I'll give him your love. Watch over his son. Julia Adorján."

Entrained the next day for Auschwitz-Birkenau, Lulu survived the journey. She even lived through the summer, fall, and winter of 1944. As some returnees from Tornalja reported, she died of typhus in Bergen-Belsen, shortly after the liberation of the camp in April 1945.

I saw my parents' despair upon reading this letter, which revealed that Lulu knew she would be taken to her death. As I mentioned, at that time most people did not know the implications of that train ride. But Lulu did. Perhaps she knew it because she had already had some experiences with people coming from the German-occupied zones of Europe, similar to mine with Hanna; or maybe because, as we were told by eyewitnesses from Tornalja after the war, she had already seen the engulfing heart of darkness when her second husband, Adolf, a famous, highly respected lawyer in Tornalja, was beaten to death in front of her by two sergeants of the Hungarian gendarmerie, who were supposed to march him and Lulu off to the ghetto. They had done this because he did not walk fast enough. Witnessing this unimaginable brutality, Lulu might have understood the future. Auschwitz? Her own death? We will never know. But there was no doubt in her mind. In fact, as her postcard reveals, she clearly knew that the goal of the journey was the murder of the Jews.

While we understood this postcard, we did not know what exactly had happened to her until much later. Nor did we know back then that Uncle Imre, my cousin Gyurika, my mother's three sisters, and their husbands were murdered that summer as well. Still, speaking with the Tevans and with others escaping from the countryside, we began to experience a constant flow of horrific news, starting in June. Yet my father never gave up hope of finding the right shelter for us, the place where all of us could hide while the gendarmes started to deport the

Jews of Budapest. And my mother? She was terrified most of the time, I think, envisioning inexorable separation, deportation, and death. Iván, on the other hand, believed in the good outcome of the war, while I practiced the piano and read a lot. I also was uncaringly happy and free at times; at others, however, I was overwhelmed by fear of separation from my parents.

1. László Abonyi

2. Margit (Nagy) Abonyi

3. Zsuzsanna and Iván Abonyi

4. Erzsébet Fajó

5. Dr. Pál Abonyi

6. Extended family group: *front:* Éva Nagy; Iván Abonyi; *middle row:* Erzsébet (Nagy) Kornél; Imre Nagy, with György Nagy in lap; Bertalan Nagy, with Zsuzsanna Abonyi in lap; Anna Nagy; *standing:* Ila (Nagy) Frank; László Kornél; Margit (Nagy) Abonyi

7. Mrs. Dobó's class, Jewish Elementary School, Békéscsaba, 1939(?): *middle row:* Zsuzsanna Abonyi (fourth from left); Márta Karácsonyi (third from right); Tomi Altmann (second from right); *seated:* Juti Bárány (second from left)

14

GHETTOIZATION

When the requirements for the registration of apartments and buildings where Jews lived had been issued back in the beginning of April, I overheard my father whispering to one of our neighbors that this process might be followed by our concentration and evacuation.

Some time passed, however, before anything happened in Budapest. One day, I remember, it was morning, shortly after my father left; I started to practice the Bach d-minor fugue from the first volume of the *Wohltemperiertes Klavier,* with Erzsi sitting next to me, listening. Suddenly I heard the familiar ringing of the doorbell and my father's voice, talking to my mother. He had obviously interrupted his routine of daily excursions, returning to discuss with us what had suddenly shocked him. He held a newspaper in his hand. Entering into what was still our library, an island as yet untouched by the destruction threatening us, he started to read aloud the section in question, in a strangely husky voice. My mother stood in the doorway. Later, she leaned against the wall. He read to us a decree that provided for the relocation and concentration of the Jews in Budapest into yellow-star houses, a decree that was issued that morning and had to be carried out right away. I stopped practicing. I understood that what I had always been frightened of had arrived; the world had taken a violent turn. It was heartbreaking to see both of my parents: my mother's face was pale, my father's desperate; he had great difficulty in formulating his words.

"This ordinance," he said slowly, "is evidence of the impending mass eviction, which," he added, repeating what he had already mentioned some time ago, "might mean nothing less than the first step toward our deportation. We need to find a place to hide!"

He fought against tears. I saw his lips forming words but his eyes reflected naked fear. Behind him, I saw Hanna's marketplace, with row upon row of the dead. It took me years before I could put together the words he whispered, citing a well-known Vörösmarty poem: "Humans are dragon-teeth, the strain / Of Man's the dragon-toothed, the race of Cain: / All hope is vain! All hope is vain!"

Erzsi sat next to me. Hugging my parents, she said over and over that no matter what happened, she would follow us wherever we were taken.

Only later did I understand that the article my father brought home gave an account of what had been an ancient, long-forgotten practice that was revitalized in Hungary in the summer of 1944: ghettoization. Indeed, the concept and practice of this measure went back to the Middle Ages. Resurrected in the spring of 1944, it was enacted all over Hungary, as it had been practiced earlier all over occupied Europe. Ghettoization helped the authorities gather and concentrate the Jews, preparing them for expulsion and mass murder. Indeed, it was from the ghetto of Tornalja that Lulu had written her last letter, and it was from the ghetto of Békéscsaba that the Tevans had fled to Budapest. Now the nightmare would take form in the capital. I was told that buildings would be designated in Budapest for this purpose, with each being individually declared a "yellow-star house," and with each displaying a huge, canary-yellow Star of David. This star was to be juxtaposed against a black background and fastened to the façade of the entrance of every single "ghetto house." Iván noted that the description of the process of turning buildings into "ghetto houses" gave a detailed explanation of the law, which declared that the selection of the "Jewish buildings" depended on the percentage of Jews living there. My father, who had already read the article, told me that most apartment houses with more than 50 percent Jews would be defined as yellow-star houses, and that these houses would then be inhabited only by Jews. Buildings that had less than 50 percent Jews as tenants were declared "Christian houses." If the Jews living in "Christian houses" had a place to move to, they were allowed to do so; if they did not, the Jewish Council assigned them a room in an apartment of one of the designated houses, one room to each family.

15

THE GHETTO HOUSE

From June 17 through June 24, about 200,000 Jews in Budapest were on the streets: moving. Getting up early the day after the decree on ghettoization was posted, my father stayed home, and we watched the hurrying masses of people from the window. Some carried their belongings in horse-drawn wagons, others in wheelbarrows, on their backs, in their hands. Marching in endless, chaotic lines, they looked harried, lonely, desperate, and, I even thought, insane. Iván and I left the house at 11:30 A.M. through a basement window. Looking back again and again, we were worried that somebody had noticed us. With a bright yellow Star of David fastened to our clothing, we stood on the corner of Abonyi Street and Aréna Street for a while, only to be followed by our parents, who had seen us leaving the house and came to usher us back to the apartment. The streets were overcrowded with police. Our parents ordered us to go back, petrified of the provocation our presence might cause in the men in uniform standing around. But then they, too, were overwhelmed by the sight they became part of on the street. Seeing old people going through the torture of pulling their carts crowded with boxes and hand-carrying their furniture, mothers with children in a breathless march, the crippled and the maimed crawling between the sidewalk and the street, my parents started to help but pulled back when they saw that a few policemen began to demand identification papers from some of the bystanders. They recoiled and shooed us away. Arriving home, I stared at the blank walls. Were we going to survive?

The measures of June 17 decreed the relocation and concentration of the Jews in the capital. Despite the fact that in our house about 70 percent of the tenants were Jews, we were not really sure whether the building would indeed become a yellow-star dwelling. I was, of course, terrified at the thought of moving. The bookshelves, our library, my piano! The work of my parents and grandparents' lives filled our apartment, and I knew it; our family often spoke of this.

Later, during the afternoon, my father said "OK," and he tried to smile, rocking me in his arms. "Objects must never be more important than life. What matters is that they don't separate us!"

"Yes," I whispered, "anything is OK, just let's stay together."

But secretly, I shivered at the thought of becoming homeless. "Homeless, homeless, homeless," I could think of nothing else. If we do not belong anywhere, we can be easily separated, I thought. Iván shrugged his shoulders and went away to work on another radio. He certainly was unwilling to discuss the threat. But my mother sobbed all night. Erzsi held me fast. She did not want to go home. My father, however, convinced her she must.

Next morning he went again to the Jewish Council. They were at work, he told us later, preparing the list of Jewish houses in Budapest. But the day after, he came home with enormously good news: our house, 10 Abonyi Street, was being designated as a yellow-star house. We were deeply relieved. We did not have to leave behind our belongings, we did not have to move. We will not be homeless, I thought, like Hanna!

But, of course, other people had to move in with us. Amid the chaos suddenly developing in the Jewish community of Budapest, by mere chance my father met somewhere a fellow pharmacist, Sanyi (Alex) Beer, whom he had known for quite a while. The Beers were looking for a place to move to, and my father was looking for people who could move into our apartment. But before any decision could be made, a question arose that needed to be answered: How many people would have to move into our apartment? Studying the case, my father found the answer. Although we had four rooms, according to police regulations in

1941, one of them did not count as a room because it just had small windows. And another room, which was very small, counted only as "half a room." As a result, our apartment was registered as a two-and-a-half-room apartment. Under the new law, there was only one room allotted to a Jewish family. In this way, the Beers fit well into our space. The four of us kept the windowless room, in addition to the room that housed the library and the Steinway, which meant in reality that we had two rooms for ourselves. My mother's room, with the "Biedermeier salon furniture," my grandfather's gift she passionately loved, became the room of Mr. and Mrs. Beer and their seven-year-old son, Jancsi (Johnny). The fourth room, a tiny place, in which Iván had lived ever since we moved to Budapest three years before, housed only a bed, a desk, and a chair. Now it became the room of Mrs. Beer's brother, Károly (Carl).

With eight people living in our apartment, we felt enormously lucky and enormously happy. First of all, my parents were relieved that "only" four more people moved in with us (most apartments in the house had now twelve to fourteen living in a space not significantly larger than ours). Second, neither Iván nor I minded the Beers or the crowdedness. In fact, I quite liked the new circumstances. I enjoyed the thought that I would have many children around to play with. I had no desire for privacy at that time; my interest in friends was significantly greater. And, of course, my parents were relieved that we did not have to leave behind, throw out, turn in, or give away our belongings, as so many people were forced to do. The poor Beers could not stay in their home. They remained with us until November 17, when we ran away from the building before it was emptied and taken over by the Arrow Cross, a gang of Hungarian National Socialists—the Nyilas. At this point we, as well as the Beers, went into hiding. And we were lucky: all of us survived the Shoah, except Károly. Drafted as a Jewish labor serviceman, he was killed on a death march led by Hungarian soldiers in the fall of 1944.

16

THE CHILDREN OF
10 ABONYI STREET

It was about noon on June 20 when the Beers appeared in the doorway of our apartment, with one of them pulling a cart, the rest carrying blankets and pillows in their hands and on their backs. They smiled kindly, but behind that smile their faces looked dark and deeply disturbed. Not five minutes passed before Mrs. Beer could no longer hide her sadness or her confusion. Her beautifully drawn face clouded with pain, her large dark eyes red, she started to sob as soon as they closed the door of their room behind themselves, and she could not stop for a long time. They seemed to be nice people, and I felt tremendously sorry for their plight.

Mr. Beer stayed with us for a little while, trying to explain that they would do everything to be good members of the household, remain strong, and survive these terrible times. They wanted, he said, to see the end of the war and, therefore, to continue to live their lives as if they had never been uprooted. We were touched by his openness and kindness, being aware of the fact that they now had a larger and heavier load to carry than we did: they had had to move; we had not. I was quite happy they came. I liked Jancsi, and I thought we would have a great time playing games. Also, I was eagerly awaiting the rest of the people moving into the building. I did not yet know what that would entail. Our apartment house had four floors, three apartments on each.

The next few days brought about changes of a magnitude that we could not even have imagined before. First of all, large numbers of people were moving into our building. Some were children, some adults; some were old, some sick, some invalid. The foyer on each floor, as well as the entrance halls of the individual apartments, were filled with groups of men, women, children, old people, furniture, packages, and personal belongings. The building looked, as my father said, like a war zone, with large groups of combatants and refugees moving back and forth, both inside and out. It took a few days before the chaos settled. Or did I just get used to it? I am not sure. But my sense of being overwhelmed, overrun, and besieged by large masses of people faded after a while. I also started to get used to the permanent change of our building's character. Its beauty and quiet elegance were gone; throngs of people filled the garden, floors, and staircases. The house took on the feel of a huge market. Its tenants changed as well: some of the older couples became more withdrawn and rarely left their apartments. Others were more sociable, while some of the new families turned out to be quite nice and friendly. In addition, a new set of children appeared, both older and younger than Iván and I, and started to play around in the backyard and the corridors.

Despite the Beers and the people living above and below us, I practiced the piano several hours a day. I also listened to the recordings of some of the great artists of the world, learning from them new phrasing, new technique, and new ways of performance. And curiously enough, despite the life-threatening events playing themselves out before our eyes, I went on practicing throughout the spring, summer, and fall of that year, until November, when we had to flee our apartment. The Beers, as well as the people above and under us, were obviously extraordinarily kind and tolerant. They never asked me to reduce my time practicing, let alone playing the piano altogether.

Soon a group of children started to get acquainted and play with one another. Of course, there were children who did not mix too much with others living in our house, but I am speaking now about a group of youngsters between the ages of nine and eighteen, who looked for one another, came together, and played together every day. Iván and I belonged among them. We even played during the night, when we were supposed to sleep, an activity that by now seemed less important to our parents to enforce as "a period of rest" than it had been before. In fact, for the moment, all rules and regulations had lost their meaning and urgency to most parents of the ghetto house. We did not have to sit down for our meals each time we ate; and nobody watched whether or not we chewed our food as we should. Neither did we have to do homework every day, nor learn French, German, or Latin words regularly, as we had had to at first when we stopped going to school in March. Now the adults were involved in things other than our training. They talked mostly to one another, trying to understand the various decrees and ordinances issued by the government; and again and again they attempted to evaluate and interpret the constantly changing stages of the war, inventing and hoping to locate ever new ways of escape. People came in and out of our apartment, held discussions with my father, and listened to the radio Iván put together. Others left the house and went out shopping, obsessed with the task of finding warm clothing or canned food for times of need, which, everybody seemed to believe, would inevitably arrive.

Never giving up the hope of escape, my father found someone who offered to take us to Romania and from there to a boat, heading toward what was then called Palestine. The person in question offered to do this for a huge amount of money, and my father considered the offer for some time. We had money. But I think he was worried about what would happen if things did not go as planned. Later he made contact with another person who also was willing to help. In fact, this one had a quite manageable plan: we should move into his house, he suggested, in Mátraháza, a resort in Hungary, where, he claimed, we could live for a thousand U.S. dollars or the equivalent thereof, paid out in advance, until the end of the war. In this case, my parents were concerned about leaving the house by car or traveling by train and about living in foreign surroundings.

In the meantime, however, we were bombarded with horror stories Erzsi and others picked up about the reaction of the police and the gendarmerie to Jews caught in hiding. One of these was my father's friend, the radiologist Mihály Fischmann, who had been in the labor service but whose wife and daughter were in Békéscsaba, trying to evade the ghetto and the ensuing deportation. They had been denounced by their neighbors, however, who had led the gendarmerie to the two women lying low in the attic of a peasant house. They had been beaten and deported just the same.

Pondering both possible escapes for some days, my parents decided against the route from Budapest to Palestine, seeing it as a terrible risk, and found the plan that would place us in a house at Mátraháza, where people would take care of us, better. But there was a problem: they had not known these people before the occupation and therefore felt they could not trust them completely. Also, the price the negotiators wanted in exchange was exorbitant. Reviewing these plans night after night (I never stopped watching the golden stream gleaming on my parents' threshold), my father decided against both and withdrew his request. At the same time, he was desperate at the thought of staying and waiting for the fulfillment of the fate the Germans designed for us. Soon he started to search for new options.

But while our parents were weighed down by the tremendous pressures created by both the daily threat and their own sense of powerlessness, the children of 10 Abonyi Street lived in a world that was different from that of the adults. In fact, amid horrific rumors, we lived in the world of fantasy, threats, fairy-tale, and imagination.

First of all, merely seeing one another meant starting to play a game that included make-believe or drama.

"Good morning, Ophelia," or "Good morning, Tristan," or "Good morning, Rigoletto," one would call out on encountering another. Picking up the game, the person so addressed would answer the call, reacting to the names of Ophelia or Tristan or Rigoletto, and starting or spinning out a scene, which then the two players either completed according to the scripts of these pieces, or invented on the spot, offering new texts and a new space for others to enter. To be able to directly continue the scripts that had been started was regarded as the greatest of all achievements.

Every day, late at night, we were told by the older children which play we would rehearse or which poem we would work on the next day. In this way, we tried to recall and learn during the night or next morning acts out of dramas or poems that were masterpieces of world literature. Or we invented plays in which these characters played leading roles, offering new performances and new experiences to one another. Whichever was the case, those playing along had to pick up and continue the pieces others (or they themselves) had started by acting out the scenes; or, if they had invented the play, they would continue to produce new texts and new sets of actions. If we were not playing, we were memorizing texts in our apartments or the corridors all day.

Another way of responding to one another was to start to draw specific rules around a highly regulated series of formal questions and answers. We invented new roles and new characters, placing them next to Romeo and Juliet or Lear and Ophelia, echoing these characters' pain or happiness or counteracting them, using a text that was similar to Shakespeare's style. Besides Shakespeare, we studied parts of, and participated in, plays of Molière, Racine, Ibsen, and Goethe, and put on performances of pieces by Karinthy, Molnár, Vörösmarty, Schiller, and Hofmannstahl. We recited Rilke's lyrics and his *Tales about God*, acted out poems by Ady, Petőfi, and Arany, and composed new plays and actions. We pretended to be imaginary characters, performing the dramas we improvised, often together with two or three other players; we recited poems by such authors as Shakespeare, Milton, and Oscar Wilde. We also wrote about and discussed books, politics, ethics, and religion, with a passion that made us inseparable from one another, a passion that forever defined our notions of play and friendship. These games shaped our world and relationships with one another, not only then and there, at that particular moment of our lives, but also for the rest of our days. In fact, later in life, most of us who were there and played with one another have tried to recreate a world of friendships and relationships similar to those we had in the ghetto house. Although the group did not stay together after the war, its magic and power on our intellectual, emotional, and creative development have been active and long-lasting, having an impact on our being and on our ways of thinking for the rest of our lives.

I became friends with Márti Elek, a beautiful twelve-year-old with dark hair, dark eyes, freckles, and funny views about the world. Iván and she fell in love with one another, and the group celebrated them as "the first young pair of our children's society." Márti had a sister, Zsuzsa, sixteen, whose blue eyes, heart-shaped face, and long, dark-blond hair made a significant impact on the boys of the yellow-star house at 10 Abonyi Street, and whose dedication to and appreciation of our games were a link in keeping the group together. And Kitty Burg, a curly-haired nine-year-old, loved my reading of *Winnie the Pooh* so much that she waited for my appearance in the foyer with this book in hand every day that summer, listening to the stories again and again. Her brother, Robi, a tall, good-looking boy with dark hair and dark eyes, was as old as Iván, and close to him as well. He played, as everybody did, but he was also very proud of his success with girls. Also Denise Vilcsek, an enormously intelligent fifteen-year-old girl, was part of the group. She hoped to become a famous writer one day. She, too, played enthusiastically with all of us, planning and explaining again and again the meaning of her beautiful short stories and poems to the group. She died of polio at the age of seventeen, a couple of years after the war. Ervin László, the twelve-year-old pianist, a *wunderkind,* another student of Faragó, played with us as well, and so did Felix Mérő, a nineteen-year-old young man who was courting Márti's sister, Zsuzsa Elek. Nonetheless, he often came just to play with the group. Then there were for a short while the Margittai children: Tomi played mostly with Iván, and Gyuri listened to my piano performances. One day, both boys disappeared with their families from the ghetto house. Gossip had it that they left Budapest on a train with some other Jews who bought their freedom from the Germans with money. After the war, we heard that they had survived, together with some 1,700 Jews who had ridden with them on the Kasztner train. I felt sad after their departure because they fit so well into our circle.

But we stayed together mostly because there was Márta Edinger, or EDMA, as she signed her artwork and cartoons in newspapers and magazines after the war, a brilliant twenty-year-old girl who became the leader of our "children's society." Turning into its organizer and the major inventor of the games we played, she also was our storyteller and theater director, in fact the poet, game-leader, jury, and judge of the group. There was no end to the stories she invented or to her reading of tales by Eichendorff, Brentano, and Rilke, in addition to her recitation of poems by Goethe, Mallarmé, Rimbaud, Verlaine, Ady, and Babits. She planned the programs the group performed and arranged the concerts given by Ervin László and me. She even helped us write the concert notes that introduced and explained the pieces we were performing. She gave talks to the children's group of 10 Abonyi Street on the great painters of the world, old and modern alike, whose works she showed around in the books she found on the bookshelves in our apartments. And she became the director of several plays we learned by heart and performed. We usually held both our rehearsals and performances in the big, comfortable foyer of the second floor of the building, bringing from the apartments for the performances chairs for the "adults," as we called our parents a bit contemptuously. The concerts in our apartment were held for a significantly smaller group of people, but with the Beers letting us take over their room and use the chairs and other pieces of furniture, we could still accommodate some fifteen to twenty people in our library room. The program notes were designed by EDMA, who made them piece after piece, using a variety of patterns and drawings as well as a number of fabulous caricatures of the people who lived in the "Jewish-House," or of the characters in the plays or political cartoons, or of all mixed together.

There can be no doubt that the world we created was above the boundaries of the ordinary, apart from the realm of politics, the war, and the future the Germans and their Hungarian partners prepared for the Jews. Ours was the world of fairy tales and games, the land of make-believe, the realm of El Dorado, which was heartbreakingly beautiful: easy to summon and impossible to resist.

In fact, these games determined the path on which the children of our group moved. Of course, our daily schedules differed. I, for example, practiced the piano in the morning, learned roles and poems in the early part of the afternoon, and threw myself into the world of games every single evening, whereas other children started to play as soon as they woke up in the morning. And while we were constantly aware of the danger threatening us, we also felt delighted by the power of these games, by the power of make-believe, by our friendship and art, and by our freedom in the world we created. Throughout the summer, leaving our apartment usually at four in the afternoon, I sat with Kitty in a corner of the staircase and read *Winnie the Pooh* to her. An essential part of our session was the last sentence of the book, which she wanted me to reread each day. This made me miraculously sad and happy alike, no matter where we stopped in the story: "But wherever they go, and whatever happens to them on the way, in that enchanted place on the top of the Forest, a little boy and his Bear will always be playing." Kitty Burg seemed to understand, as all of us did that summer, that if we wanted, we could leave this world behind and could act as if we were living in another one that was ruled by games. Kitty loved us to act out some of the book's scenes, and promised me again and again that she would play for ever, even when she grew up, just as Pooh and Christopher Robin would continue to play. At that time, I was not aware of the reason for our passionate desire for our games; nor, I am sure, did the others know why we did it. But later I recognized that in these games, we found a space that allowed us to leave behind the world of the "the adults" as well as the ghetto house and with it the Germans, our fear of separation, and the threat of death.

After I finished reading Kitty a new section from *Winnie the Pooh*, we looked for the rest of the group. We usually found them somewhere in the house, and we started to play immediately.

Somebody always asked, even before we agreed which game we would start out the night with, "Who will ask the questions?"

"I will."

"I will."

"I will," each of us volunteered in turn.

Whoever had that role could decide what kind of a game we would play. If it was not theater, one child would leave, while the rest agreed on a particular task, such as, for example, figuring out the person the group had in mind.

Returning, the child would ask, "What kind of flower would he or she be?"

"A rose!" someone screamed.

"No," argued another. "A violet."

"Not me," said a third person. "I agree with the first answer; although I see there lilies as well."

"OK. What kind of a river? A fast one?"

"No."

"A quiet, lovely one?"

"Yes."

"Well, I don't agree," someone would say. "I see the person more as a glittery rivulet."

"And I," yet another would chime in, "perceive her as a stream at times, running among flowery fields at others, stretching out as a silvery ribbon."

"And what kind of a composer would he or she be? . . ."

"And what color? . . ."

"And what instrument? . . ."

And so it went on and on, until an unmistakable profile would emerge of the person around whom the children's game revolved, and the boy or girl asking the question could name the figure.

This was my favorite game. Years, even decades later, I still ask myself when thinking of someone, "What kind of plant would this person be?"

"What kind of dish?"

"What kind of painter?"

But other children liked "Bar Kokhba," a clever, tightly moving question-and-answer game, which required a group selecting a notion, character, or object, and a person figuring out the answer. At other times, the group acted out the ways in which an individual would behave or write or speak, all of which were clues given to the person's identity, and one had to attempt to figure out whom the group had in mind. There were endless poems and plays the group acted out at times to people whose task was to name the piece by listening to the texts or the details of a scene. And there were new games, every day.

The summer moved slowly. The war, of course, with our fate tied to it, was at the center of everything we did or thought of. But the children's group was free of the life-and-death struggle of the grown-ups. We played.

17

A MIRACLE

Suddenly, at the end of June, the world turned dark. Doomsday, it seemed, loomed near, with bad news circling around the ghetto house. At first, I noticed that my father and Iván were constantly whispering to one another; sometimes they talked in a low voice to my mother as well. Then Erzsi seemed to be busier than ever before, having less time to talk to me, speaking constantly of the urgency of finding a hiding place for us all. At this point, however, I decided to disregard the "news" as well as Erzsi's plans. I distanced myself from the "real world," or, as we called that senseless, brutal place in our children's group, "the realm of the adults"— continuing to play make-believe. Just as I had done earlier, in third grade, when I first heard about Hanna's marketplace, I kept myself away from the news. But I could not avoid hearing about the huge concentration of the gendarmerie troops around Budapest nor keep myself away from the whirling rumors regarding the official attention that turned, as we now know, to the immediate entrainment of the Jews in the capital. Of course, as soon as I was brutally confronted with what *might* come, it was no longer possible to run away from the news. Starting to listen to it, I understood that most people thought we would be deported at the beginning of July. It took some days before I admitted to myself that the moment I had dreaded for years had arrived. And I knew it would destroy our lives.

Soon it became obvious that everybody expected the worst. My father's beautiful, intelligent, warmly glowing dark eyes grew deeper and larger. My mother cried all the time. "My children! My two beautiful children! And we have nowhere to go!" she kept on repeating.

Also the Beers appeared heavily burdened, silently moving around the house, carefully closing the doors behind themselves. I stopped practicing. I stopped reading as well, and I even stopped briefly playing make-believe with my friends. We still met at night, but there was not much we talked about. Nor did the adults argue or spend time with one another. It seemed that everybody lost interest in interacting, planning, working, or preparing for something important. Suddenly, out of this paralysis, a state of panic took over. Mrs. Nagy, one of our neighbors who lived on the fourth floor and had two children, a little girl about six years old and a boy of fifteen with Down syndrome, came to visit my mother.

"I won't allow them to separate me from my children," she said over and over.

Obviously she was terrified of the arrival of the Hungarian gendarmerie, whose murderous treatment of Jews in the ghettos located in the countryside was by the end of June fully known in Budapest. But she had no idea about the purpose of the journey she would be forced to undertake nor about her "freedom of decision" regarding her children. In fact, she did not know and could not foresee what we learned only after the end of the war: that if by some miracle she and her children had survived the train trip, all of them would have been gassed in Auschwitz upon arrival. For the story of Auschwitz was still kept secret from the Jews of Budapest in June 1944.

Still, whatever had happened in the ghetto house until now was different from a new sense of danger just settling in among its people. The days passed slowly; we mostly stayed inside our apartments. Then suddenly, amid this sense of dread and terror, amid this tense expectation of a storm, my mother started to speak to me about a threat that was in sight, emphasizing that I was a big girl now and must, therefore, understand the problems we were facing. That is, I must know that perhaps, sometime, before the end of the war, I would have to hide somewhere without her and my father, without Iván and Erzsi. This meant, she said, that I would have to live alone for a while perhaps, have another name, and act as if I were someone other than Zsuzsi Abonyi, the person I really was. Or, perhaps, I would have to live together with other children or adults I had not known before, in places I had never yet been. In addition, she said, maybe sometime she or Iván or my father would have to do the same. That we should do so, however, was of great importance for our future, because if we were successful, we could avoid deportation. She insisted on the significance of our attempts to stay alive and being grateful for having found secure hiding places. Emphasizing the moral goal of the task of survival, she maintained that we must do everything to make sure that nobody recognized us and found out who we really were. When everything was over, she tried to assure me, we would find one another and from that time onward, we would live happily ever after.

Each time she started speaking about this, I would be crying before she finished. She became desperate, and so did my father. What could they have done with me? I behaved terribly. I did not seem to understand that they needed my cooperation, that our separation was imminent, and so was the need for my pretense of being someone other than the little Jewish girl I was. We would not survive otherwise. But I did not want to hear about it. I did not want to be alone; I did not even want to *act* as if I were alone. After several attempts, they looked around and reached out for what appeared to them a wonderful idea, one that would, they hoped, eliminate my resistance. They decided to use make-believe to overcome my fear of separation. They thought of my enjoyment of the children's group and about our games of acting out strange scenes, identifying with a variety of characters. My mother started to propose that we play a game in which she would act as a fictitious lady in the apartment where I had just arrived. And I would play the role of a girl from the countryside in search of her parents, who had just moved to Budapest, leaving her with her grandparents. But the grandparents had died, and now she had come to Budapest to find her mother and father. At that time, the countryside, especially in eastern Hungary, where the Soviet troops, we were told, were soon going to arrive and push westward and northward, was in disarray, producing tens of thousands of refugees in Budapest. Indeed, the capital was full of strangers and even children, abandoned by or separated from their parents, who had come from the countryside. My parents thought these throngs of people and their tales would strengthen my story, which, in turn, would allow me to remain secure wherever I was in hiding. What they could not foretell, however, was how poorly I would be able to use this story as the frame for my life, how well and for how long I could play the role of Zsuzsi Ákom (this was the name that appeared on my false birth certificate; this was the persona whose identity I would now have to assume). To ease my situation, my mother wanted me to practice the hiding game. But I did not want to play it. I looked to my father for help. He tried to encourage me to play along. And when he noted my unwillingness, he left the room; I saw that there were tears in his eyes. I called him back and started to play. It was both a boring and a very frightening game.

The real problem was, however, that no matter how often we went back and forth, trying to pretend again and again, my parents were dissatisfied with me. I was not convincing enough, they thought. Where was my "great talent," which they had recognized when I appeared in various plays, acting out a variety of roles? As if possessed by the idea, Erzsi as well as my mother tried to "practice" this game with me. They wanted me to play the role of Zsuzsanna Ákom. They believed that if I had some practice, I would feel more comfortable in the skin of this "other girl" and would be more able to move around in the new surroundings all by myself. We did play this game a few times, but I hated it.

In the meantime, in the world of high politics, big changes were taking place. While the reports of the atrocities committed by the Hungarian gendarmerie and the police in the countryside became known to the Jewish community of Budapest, the news regarding the mass killings of the Jews in the concentration camps of German-occupied Poland also started to reach members of the government. As we learned later, the regent had known this long before the first trains of Hungarian Jews arrived in Auschwitz-Birkenau. But now he could feign ignorance no longer. Confronted with the gruesome details of the Vrba report—the eyewitness account of the two young men who had escaped from Auschwitz—Horthy started to pay attention to the issue. By the middle of June, these reports reached the Western press. And by the end of June, after the Allies had already liberated southern Italy, Pope Pius XII, who had previously never raised his voice on behalf of the Jews, sent a cable to Horthy appealing their deportation to the concentration camps. Soon thereafter, President Roosevelt warned the regent of the consequences the deportation of the Budapest Jews would bring to Hungary. The American president's letter was followed by a letter from the Swedish king and by communications from other governments. In addition to these letters, an exceptionally heavy air raid was unleashed against Budapest on July 2. I remember that air raid. It was on my birthday. We ran to the attic to see the bombs falling. Even though our house was shaking, Iván and I, and a number of other children as well as many adults, watched the attack with tremendous hope. The bombs exploded, and the sky was black, with orange flames and dark smoke surging through the air. Huge detonations made the house leap; and the blasts thundered in our ears. But we were not afraid. Quite the opposite. Even the youngest among us knew, whether or not we would live to see it, that liberation and freedom from terror and murder were on the way.

As I learned later, Horthy's reaction to that air raid was immediate and energetic. It came just at a time when several countries' heads of state were protesting the deportation of the Jews, and when the military reality was foretelling the collapse of the Third Reich more clearly than ever. On July 7, he decided to act. While the gendarmerie and the police prepared to start the forced transport of more than 200,000 Jews in Budapest, Horthy suspended the operation. First of all, he fired the two major executors of the "de-Jewification process," László Baky and László Endre, both secretaries of state in the Ministry of the Interior, and thereby halted the transfer of Jews to the concentration camps. Despite pressure from the German and Hungarian sides, he did not give in. The deportation of the Jews of Budapest did not take place for the time being. In fact, it remained suspended throughout the summer of 1944.

We, of course, hoped that it had been called off forever. But we were unsure. Unaware of exactly what had happened, we were afraid of the resumption of the deportation process at any moment. In fact, for several days after July 2, we were still trembling. And time dragged on. Numb and in despair, we stayed in the apartment. And since we did not know what was taking place in the background, we feared we were not yet over the danger. My sole concern was my father: I could think of nothing else but of him: What am I going to do if we are separated? If they kill him? I could not look at him without crying, but I did not want him to see me in despair. Still, I hid my dread from everyone, even from Erzsi, whose words remained floating around me forever: "Wherever they take you, I'll come along."

"You know what?" said my father one day. "I think we won't be taken anywhere. At least not now. It appears that they have cancelled the deportation."

Erzsi started sobbing.

Later, when we were alone, Erzsi held my hand: "I went to church on your birthday," she said. "I prayed so hard! And I heard what God told me! Did you know that? He was talking to me!"

"And what did he say?" I asked, my mouth open, my amazement immense.

"He promised me that none of us will be deported!"

"And what about Pali and Anni?" I pulled the rug from under her feet.

"I cannot know everything," she snapped. She was annoyed.

The night went by; so did the next day, and the next few weeks. The Jews of Budapest were not deported to Auschwitz.

It took some time before we recovered from the shock. And when we did, we started to fall back into the pattern of our usual life. The children's group resumed playing. I was Nanerl, Mozart's sister, one day, and Clara Schumann the next. I also played a role in a Karinthy piece:

I was the clown. Our performances were enormously successful! Some adults recommended that I be an actress when I grew up. Indeed, that was my second choice; I still preferred to become a pianist. But the girl my parents wanted me to play I never wanted to be.

Suddenly more news arrived: Romania sued for an armistice on August 23, 1944, and the Soviet troops, finally, neared the Hungarian border. Iván explained to me that Horthy had made changes in his government: he had replaced several of its most anti-Semitic members. The life of the Jews became a hair easier and quite a bit more hopeful. Even my father was laughing again. And the children of 10 Abonyi Street started to play more intensely than ever before. The sessions were in full swing by noon, going until midnight.

August passed and so did September. With the Allies moving ahead on the western and the eastern fronts alike, the end seemed nearer every day. Still, fearing the possibility of "last-minute" excesses, Erzsi and my father made sure that the hiding places they had got for us earlier in the summer were still functional. Our false papers were in place, and Erzsi agreed with the people willing to hide us for enormous sums of money that they would be notified at the time of need. At this point, the question was only *when* my father would decide was *the right moment*. Or should we go right now, leaving behind everything we owned, everything and everybody we knew, bringing ill-fate upon the Beers and our neighbors? For if we disappeared, my parents thought, Mrs. Henk, the caretaker, would notice our absence and report it to the police. They would want to investigate the case, accusing perhaps the Beers and others of conspiracy. Also, should we give up one another and move in with strangers, to places where the neighbors might become suspicious and denounce us? Or should we wait and just lie low under the given circumstances? For how long should we do so? And what if we waited too long and could no longer get away at the last moment? That is, should we wait until things got worse? Of course, the real question was: Will we have time to flee when "things got worse"? There can be no doubt that all of these decisions had serious, long-lasting consequences. And my parents were desperately undecided as to which one to choose.

Erzsi still came to us every day throughout the summer, bribing the caretaker each time she rang the doorbell. She helped my mother and everybody else in the house; she played cards with me and Iván; she also read to me. And we played make-believe as we had always done. Sometimes she joined in the games of the "children's group" as well. Loved by everybody, she played along passionately. And she was excellent at everything, except in learning roles. She did not like to memorize texts for performances, nor did she want to act before an audience—while the rest of us loved to do so. Otherwise, she did not change: she was at times more thoughtful and a bit more tense than before, though.

In the meantime, the Soviet forces arrived at the Hungarian border, crossing it on October 6. By October 14 they had forced their way through a passage over the Tisza River. The march against Budapest was under way. And with the Allies penetrating the German lines, the end of the war was in sight..

18

THE RETURN OF HORROR

Then came October 15. It was around noon, I remember, and I had just started to practice Bach's c-minor prelude and fugue, trying to play the prelude staccato, or at least not legato, searching for ways to recreate the percussive sound of the harpsichord on the piano. Suddenly Iván flung open the door. Behind him I saw my father's pale face and my mother's clutched hands held up in the air. From the left, the Beers rushed into the room. Some neighbors appeared as well, some just coming through the door, others ringing the doorbell. The people of the ghetto house had heard that something was happening. Knowing that we had a functional radio, they gathered in our apartment. Some of them sat down in a chair, others on the floor. A few stood erect or leaned against the wall. There must have been twenty to twenty-five people in the room. Several of them were crying.

On the radio, Horthy was speaking. A tense, mesmerized audience listened to his words, their eyes and mouths open. He announced the news: he was suing for peace.

"It's obvious to every thinking person that Germany has lost this war," he declared. "Aware of my historical role, I must do everything to stop the ongoing destruction."

"God! But what will the Germans do now?" asked most people in the room of one another. They seemed to be shaken, overwhelmed by both fear and happiness.

"If Hungary resists the Germans," said Mr. Beer, "the Germans will bomb Budapest and kill everyone they regard as their enemy. Not to speak about us, the Jews! So it's obvious that they will resume the deportations."

"Yes. But the Germans are not that powerful anymore," said my father. He seemed truly optimistic now. "They are suffering from the certainty of their own defeat; and, in the end, they know they have but a short time left. On all fronts, they are losing, and the Allies are marching on, ready to wipe them out. There can be no doubt that the Germans are enormously concerned about their future. They are not going to squander their troops on us and on Horthy."

This sounded very logical, our visitors agreed. They did not yet know what I learned only much later: namely, that for the Germans and their Hungarian supporters, the war against the Jews was of primary concern, more important than the war they had started against the Allies, more important than their children's future. In fact, these people would rather lose the war than give up murdering the Jews. Our guests stayed around for a while, talking about the details of Horthy's speech; while most were happy and relieved, others saw the new developments as potentially catastrophic.

Then the doorbell rang. It was Gyuri Faragó. I gazed at him incredulously, barely recognizing him. He had lost much weight since I had last seen him, perhaps a month or so before. He had been a slender man, but now he was skin and bone, his handsome face covered with a yellowish glaze, his intelligent, blue eyes tempered.

"I fear," he said, "that things might become difficult right now. I don't think you should stay here. After all, you could hide in our apartment. In fact, I came to pick up Zsuzsi for a few days and anybody else who wants to join us. I don't think it's a very good idea to stay here. The backlash is on its way. The Nyilas will take over!"

"I don't want to go!" I objected. But my parents wanted me to leave, and Erzsi promised she would come soon after. They put on me a hat and coat, and before I knew it, I had left the house with Faragó. We did not talk: I was struggling not to cry, and he did not know what to say.

Arriving at his apartment, we sat down in the piano room. I regained my voice and wanted to talk about something other than what was happening. Starting to formulate ideas, I had heard from my father about the development of polyphony. I wanted to discuss Bach with him. But we did not. He could not pay any attention to me because his telephone rang every other second. Friends kept calling him, obviously out of fear for their future. Careful of what he said, suspecting his phone was being tapped, he used sub rosa expressions, which I understood because, in the past, I had often overheard my parents talking this way over the telephone. While offering his apartment to one family, he helped and gave advice to everyone who called. It was enormously moving to listen to him. I knew that I was witnessing something great and heroic, feeling proud of him, having him as our friend. Yet I noticed during these discussions that he was exhausted and in pain, although he tried to control his voice and kept on speaking calmly about various avenues his friends could now undertake in order to hide.

While deeply in awe of his care, love, and courage, I spent the afternoon in terrible fear for my parents. I was expecting them and Iván, or at least Erzsi, to arrive. But they did not come. And we could not communicate through a telephone; Faragó had a functioning one, but my parents did not. I felt hopelessly cut off from them. My heart beating wildly, I waited for Erzsi's call, but she did not call or come. Sitting there for hours and waiting for something to happen, I became more and more upset, until I noticed that there was a new voice speaking on the radio. In fact, it soon became obvious that there was something important happening. Mrs. Faragó came into the room and stood by the door; Gyuri sat up in his bed, although he appeared to be terribly weak. They listened to the radio. He waved me to come closer and sit in a chair next to his bed. I did so. From the radio a new voice resounded. It was Ferenc Szálasi, leader of the Arrow Cross Party, who was speaking.

He said, "The world is burning, its flames threaten to engulf Hungary." And he called on every Hungarian "to work on putting out the fire."

Blaming the Jews "for their responsibility for this catastrophe," he promised "to finish the work started and rid the country of this insidious enemy." All of us knew that he meant to restart and complete the deportation of the Jews—more precisely, the Jews in Budapest.

It was strange to listen to him. I registered not only the hatred pouring out of his voice and the hatred driving his plans but also his bombastic words and cheap rhetoric. Still, the process he spoke of had consequences obviously broader than just linguistic. With his slogans and insane promises about winning the war, which everybody whom I knew considered impossible, with his brutal threats and demands, he and his party initiated a period in Hungarian history that added six additional months to the country's involvement in World War II, caused the deaths of more than 150,000 people, and created a dominion of terror in which additional tens of thousands of Jews were murdered.

Listening to this speech, I felt terribly threatened. Until this moment, I had not heard many hate speeches on the radio. But this one was frightening. I felt attacked. And my parents were not there with me! Sitting in an armchair, I cried. Although I loved being with the Faragós, I longed for my parents. I wanted to go home. Outside was dark. Gyuri sat in bed, his skin dark yellow in the light of the lamp. He looked like someone in great pain, anguish in his eyes, his lips parched, a grimace distorting his face. His nightgown hung on what appeared to be the mere bones of his shoulders; he looked emaciated.

"He is going to die," I thought, and shook with cold and fear. My stomach cramped. "No, no, no, he won't!" a voice argued with me. "He will live, and we'll celebrate the day of liberation together!" I didn't believe that voice: "Not even *I* can face up to truth, even *I* want to live with a liar inside me," I thought.

Then the bell rang, and Erzsi came in, her face covered with cold sweat. I begged her to take me home, and she said she would. Embracing Faragó hurt me deeply because I thought I would never see him again. I was right; I never did. He stroked my hair; his hand seemed small and thin, his skin transparent. We left, but I looked back from the door and captured once more his anguished smile and the blueness of his eyes. I thought that he was already above us, in the sky.

The streets were dark and completely deserted. I no longer remember how late it was. But Erzsi told me, and I could feel her tremble as she held my arm, that there was a general curfew after 5:00 P.M. I knew that the war was in its last phase now, yet the Arrow Cross ran all over the place, hunting for Jews. Erzsi had my false papers in her purse. If we were to be stopped and had to show our identification papers, I must, she whispered, say that I am Zsuzsanna Ákom, that I come from Békéscsaba, and that she, Erzsi, is my relative. She grabbed my arm as we crossed the streets. I walked close to her, my heart about to burst. I expected the Arrow Cross to stop us any minute. But they were not around; the streets were empty. Arriving at our house, we went through the iron gate, turned to the side garden, and climbed through a window Erzsi had left open in the basement because we did not dare to come through the main door. Ringing the doorbell, she feared, would alert the caretaker.

The door to our apartment was unlocked. I stepped inside and threw myself into my parents' arms. I was home. Making scrambled eggs for me, they were amazed at my enormous appetite. Still, the question that needed to be discussed at this point was not my hunger, but our next move. Talking about it back and forth, I recognized that my parents were just as undecided now as before. I knew that we could not stay much longer at 10 Abonyi Street, because, I clearly understood, staying meant essentially waiting for the Nyilas. At the same time, my parents were afraid of leaving the house. They worried that we would be stopped and shot on sight. Indeed, they knew that there were constant raids by the police and the Nyilas in Budapest, in the streets, in train stations, on buses, and on streetcars: everywhere. Not even with false papers, they felt, should we try to go out into the darkness of the night, especially not the four of us together. Listening to their arguments for a while, I fell asleep.

19

EVIL TIDINGS

A loud discussion between my mother, my father, and Erzsi next morning woke me up, making it clear to me that they thought we must flee immediately and find a place to hide. Erzsi left hurriedly, but she returned within a few hours bringing bad news. Most people who had offered their dwellings to us during the summer were not around any more; they had left for the countryside or moved to other addresses. There was only one couple she had found at home during her search, but, she said, they told her that they were now frightened of their neighbors and therefore unwilling to let Jews move into their apartment.

Still, Erzsi did not feel defeated. She said she believed what my father maintained, that the task was easier at this point in the war than it had been during the spring or summer of this year. While the danger was greater, as the Nyilas pulled together their forces to eliminate the remaining Jews in Budapest, the end was closer. The Allies were already fighting in Germany, and the Soviet army was marching toward Budapest; the end of the regime, my father maintained, was a question of a couple of months rather than years.

"It won't last long," he said again and again.

Quite optimistically, Erzsi went out on a search the next day. To no avail: she came back empty-handed. It was October 17. She went out to search on October 18 as well. Finally, on October 19, she located a person who offered his help. She and my father decided to go back to visit him once more, the next day. That visit did not take place, however, for on that day, something happened that was worse than any of my nightmares, worse than my fears of Hanna's marketplace, worse than my decision to take my life: the Arrow Cross came, picked up my father, and marched him off to a camp.

We woke up at 6:00 A.M. to a horrible scream. We ran to the entrance hall; peeking through the keyhole, my father saw that several of the Nyilas were racing through the staircase of the house, rifles slung from their shoulders. We ran back to the inside of the apartment, but could not help hearing as they shot their way inside some apartments. Those doors on our floor, including ours, they just kicked in or tore open, yelling, "Every man between sixteen and fifty, every woman between sixteen and forty-five, get ready! Hurry downstairs!"

"Wake up, you lazy lot! Out of bed! Every decent Hungarian is at work, but you are asleep, damn Jews!"

"Wake up! Wake up! The time for being a bum is over!"

"Men between sixteen and fifty, out of bed."

"Out of bed, swines!"

"You must be at the entrance of the house by 6:15; if you are not, we will come, get you, and shoot you dead!"

"We have the list of names in our hands! We know who you are! If you don't appear downstairs in fifteen minutes, we'll find you in your apartment."

Iván did not fall into the age group they came to drive away, neither did I or my mother. My father did. Dressing and hurrying up, he reached for the backpack prepared by my mother a couple of days before. I ran into the room and threw myself on his bed. It was still warm. His face in anguish, he bent over me. Iván came in too. In a hurry, my father kissed us and left. We went after him to the foyer.

"If any of you damned Jews follow these swines, we'll shoot you on sight," a tall, strong man with a pockmarked face screamed at us.

I ran back and again threw myself on my father's bed. Now it felt cold.

Then I ran to the window. Carefully watching from behind the curtain, Iván and I observed a growing group of about forty to fifty men, standing on the street, forming rows of five. And there were women in another group, but farther to the right.

"The marketplace," I thought to myself, recognizing clearly that the image of my nightmares had now materialized: "He had promised me that they wouldn't do this in Hungary," I sobbed.

But Iván hissed at me, "Are you nuts or what? You are making it harder for him."

My mother tried to smile down from the window at my father. "We must be strong," she said to me, "terribly strong." But she turned away, crying.

While several screaming Nyilas ran in and out of our house and the neighboring house as well (a ghetto house just like ours), I understood that within the next few minutes the men of both houses would be marched away. Watching my father's group from the window, we saw that they were just staring at one another or looking at the ground. But occasionally, as if it were just by chance, my father would raise his eyes, and in so doing he intimated to me that he would return.

It took probably a good half an hour, amid the screaming of the Nyilas, until the group was ordered to march off. I thought I caught my father's last glance before he left. But he did not wave. We heard a guard scream, "If you wave, I'll shoot you!"

I felt as if they had torn out my heart. Everything I had ever been afraid of had now come true. I sobbed and trembled. Lying on the top of his bed, I hoped this was a dream. But it was not. And nobody could help me. Nobody even tried. My mother was devastated; she could not speak; it was she who needed help. And Iván disappeared. I think he, too, was crying somewhere. Then, after a while, clearly and distinctly, I heard the voice of my father: "I'll return!"

I listened. Thinking back on those hours, I remember, I did not consider suicide. In fact, recalling that day, I remember that that whole idée fixe that had occupied me for years had vanished. It was as if everything I had known and thought about the brutal separation from my parents before the Germans occupied Hungary culminated in my mind on the day they arrived. Afterward, it lost its power over me. How could I commit suicide without him? How could I leave him? He must find me when he returns. Although the worst had taken place and he had been taken away, I did not think of dying. Rather, while I cried in despair and was paralyzed with pain, I repeated again and again to myself that he would return.

Later that morning Erzsi arrived. She broke out in a terrible wail when she heard what had happened. After a while, she stopped sobbing, however, and agreed with my mother that we must live and act as if he were still with us. That meant she must find some reliable hiding places for us, because the lack of them made us terribly vulnerable. We could be picked up at any time by the Nyilas, killed, or sent on death marches toward Austria. Yet we dared not leave our apartment before we knew where to go, because the streets were dangerous as well, with the police and the Nyilas constantly rounding up people everywhere. Also, we were frightened about moving into a strange environment. As we knew from rumors circulating in Budapest, if a neighbor denounced a person in whose apartment Jews were hiding, the Nyilas would come and shoot on sight those they found there or take them to the Danube and shoot them into the river. Although by then deportations to Auschwitz had stopped (by late fall, Romania, Poland, and even parts of eastern Hungary were liberated by the Soviet forces), death marches were undertaken on the roads west from Budapest, toward the camps in Austria and Germany.

For the moment, Erzsi and my mother decided to stay put in the ghetto house until Erzsi found a better solution. Despite her awareness of the danger of remaining in this place, my mother was simply too frightened to leave our apartment and go with us to strangers, about whom she knew nothing, whom she did not trust. But by the end of October, staying in the house had become precarious. As for my friends, most of them had fled with their parents, leaving everything behind, looking for other quarters. In fact, just a few days after my father was marched away, our original group of children shrank significantly; only four kids—Kitty, Robi, Iván, and I—remained in the ghetto house. And there were other significant changes. With the Russians approaching the capital, our food supply had suddenly become scarce. In addition, the shelling of Budapest had begun. In the embattled city, as rumors had it, the Nyilas had started to break into the ghetto houses, marching away the Jews who could walk and murdering the rest.

Our life hung now on a slender thread. My father's absence drove my mother into despair. She was frightened, helpless, and lonely, crying often, holding me in her arms. Iván, on the other hand, showed tremendous strength. He not only preoccupied himself all day with assembling and installing new radios and a record player, but he also listened to the news and reported the events of the front to the rest of the people in the ghetto house, keeping them aware of every detail of the war. In addition, he listened to music, learning to love more pieces of the classical repertoire. As time passed, I started to practice again, still learning more Bach preludes and fugues and studying several Beethoven sonatas. And at night, with ever-growing interest, I began to read some of the great novels of the nineteenth and twentieth centuries. In fact, I finally had the freedom to read without parental supervision works by Dickens, Victor Hugo, Zola, Balzac, and Thomas Mann. I was also writing a diary, and playing a game by myself, pretending that my father was at home. We told stories to one another, arguing and laughing during the day as well as during the night. Sometimes my mother joined me in playing this game as well, or she would talk to me about him. And again and again, the two of us would pray for his life.

Then, one day, Erzsi arrived with a letter in her hand. We recognized it immediately. But I could not believe my eyes: it was in my father's handwriting. He had written to her—for Jews were not allowed to use the mail system—using a double entendre by which we understood he was in a camp near Gödöllő, a town east of Budapest. He was working, he wrote, in an army pharmacy, where, as we learned later, he was responsible for the medication of an army division as well as of the labor servicemen. This was wonderful news. It told us that he was still alive and that he would resist the blows; in fact, it let us know that he would come back. This thought did not leave me for a second. Having read the letter a thousand times over, I stood on the bed under the window, watching the street constantly; I was waiting and waiting for him. But he did not come. Then I started to cry in my mother's arms, noticing that she and Erzsi grew more upset every day. The hours passed, he did not come. After a while, I could neither read nor practice.

One afternoon, during the first days of November, someone rang the doorbell. Thinking it was a neighbor visiting my mother, I ran to the door and opened it. But it was he who stood in the door frame, a broad smile on his face, wearing his dark blue cashmere coat and his gray hat, just as he had done when he left.

"I told you," he said, tears in his eyes. "I told you that I would return."

I could not even scream. In the next second, I, my mother, and Iván were in his arms, sobbing! Now I knew I was *not* dreaming, I was *not* playing. I squeezed his hands for the next two days. I knew he was here! But he had to go back, he said, as did the other two physicians he had left the camp with. They came, he emphasized, officially. Indeed, they had been sent to Budapest by their commandant, a good and decent man, to pick up some medicine from the main military hospital. How my father arranged the rest, I do not know. But he came home: he held me in his arms, discussed the necessity of a hiding place with Erzsi and my mother, and argued with all of us regarding his decision to return to the camp he had just come from. Indeed, while everybody thought it was senseless, even suicidal, to go back to the camp, he claimed that there were no options because he had promised the commander who had let him go that he would return. If he or the others he came with did not return, he said, the lives of the rest of the labor servicemen would be endangered. For this reason, he insisted, he could not stay. But he promised again and again that on the very next occasion, he would escape and return to us.

It was early in the morning when he left. The two colleagues with whom he had left the camp came to pick him up. I ran after him on the staircase, but I was not allowed to go outside. He had permission to do so; I did not. He would be very upset, he said, if I followed him. I went with him to the door. A last embrace. I scaled the stairs and ran back to the window of our apartment; the three men were walking slowly away. The sun rays lit up the color of his dark blue coat. Wearing his gray hat, and marching with his two colleagues on either side, he disappeared in the light. I felt as if the buildings and trees around them were shaking. I lay down on my bed. I was falling.

20

TOGETHER

The days passed. The weather got colder. One day Erzsi came home; she was out of breath. She had just met one of my father's contacts, who was a member of the Zionist Hehalutz organization. He convinced her to go to the Nunciature and stand in line for "protective passes," which he said the Vatican had just started to issue, and which the Hungarian Arrow Cross government had just decided to recognize. I learned only much later about the background of these rapidly developing changes. The initiative came from a truly humane, compassionate man, Angelo Rotta, the apostolic nuncio and dean of the diplomatic corps in Hungary, who became involved in the struggle for the lives of Budapest Jews. He started to issue them papers of "safe conduct" and requested in November 1944 that the Hungarian government recognize their protection with a Vatican pass.

While we did not know the background of these passes, nor the circumstances under which they were issued, nor even the fact that many of them were being falsified by young Jews, members of various Zionist organizations, we were very much aware of the fact that we would be greatly helped by possessing such a document. So we anxiously waited for Erzsi's return. When she got back, she entered the apartment with papers in hand that claimed we were under the protection of the Vatican. Filled out for us, "László Abonyi and his family," and signed by Angelo Rotta, this pass became the key to life for the four of us, the means to escape separation, torture, and death. After months of searching for ways of rescue, we finally had something that made our escape possible: a pass the Nyilas would recognize.

There was only one problem: our father had not returned yet. Of course, the pass could possibly bring him home. But how to find him? What to do? Aware of the Nyilas' attempts at murdering the remaining Jews, we started to fear the worst, for we knew about the death marches. Some people were lucky enough to flee from them. Returning to Budapest, they told stories that were filled with accounts of starvation, cruelty, death, and torture. We were desperate. What I hoped with Iván, though, was that our father would stay in Gödöllő, under the command of that decent man who had sent him to Budapest a few weeks before. But our hopes were in vain; and we were still quite ignorant of the decision of the Germans and their Hungarian allies to murder *every Jew* still alive or to take them out of the country. Our father did not stay in Gödöllő. One day Erzsi came home with a new postcard. Its message, too, had a double meaning, but a less reassuring message than the previous one: it gave account of his "enjoyment of the countryside," including the long walks he was taking toward the western provinces.

"My God! They are taking him on a death march to Austria!" my mother cried, her face turning white.

She was right. This is what the postcard was all about. We were helpless. Although I prayed and prayed and prayed all day that he would escape, I knew that time had turned against us. And as the war came closer, the persecution of the Jews became more savage every day. At times I feared that he would never come home and that, in the end, all of us would be killed. Feeling more and more abandoned, I gave Erzsi a letter I had recently written to Faragó, telling him about my father's draft into slave labor service, my loneliness, and my questions about Chopin's last prelude in d minor. Obviously I needed to talk to somebody. He wrote me back a sweet note that gave me the impetus to practice several hours. Otherwise, I read most of the time. I also knew that we would not remain in the house for long. But I shivered when I heard people speaking about leaving.

"We will be homeless," I told Erzsi.

"But we won't be homeless for long," said my mother, her face quite pale and, suddenly, old. "Everything will be here, waiting for our return." And desperately she tried to smile. I wanted so much to believe her!

Suddenly, one afternoon, there was a huge commotion outside our apartment. With our eyes at the keyhole, we saw again the Nyilas, with rifles slung from their shoulders, screaming and running back and forth, making a large crowd of women move on and press up the staircase, ordering some to settle down in the foyer and the stairs, while chasing others up to the third and fourth floors. It turned out later that they wanted to put them up for the night in our still-existing ghetto house, only to drive them on next morning. Ringing the doorbells, banging or kicking in the doors of every apartment, they demanded that we open our doors for the newcomers, who needed to use our toilets. We learned later that these prisoners had been picked up from various ghetto houses, while their families had been left behind in the apartments whence they had been snatched. It was difficult to talk with them, however. They were panic-stricken and horrified, begging us to find ways in which to communicate with their families. Erzsi took a number of addresses; later, she even found some of these women's family members. But her help was just a drop in the bucket. They needed more than what she could offer. I did not sleep much that night. And when I did, I saw my father in my dreams. I begged him to come home; I begged him to escape.

Next day, the group of 100 to 150 women was marched off from our house. What happened to them? Were they taken on a death march toward Austria? Or perhaps shot somewhere in Budapest? Into the Danube? I do not know! I have never found anybody who was in the group that was marched to 10 Abonyi Street on November 15, 1944, or met anybody who knew what happened to these unfortunate women.

The day after the women were driven out of our ghetto house, on November 16, I sat down early in the morning to try to read *Les Misérables*. Later, Erzsi arrived, but instead of playing with me, she started to speak about the importance of accepting my role as an orphan, were I now forced to move somewhere by myself. Before I could answer her, the bell rang. Running to the door, I yanked it open. Suddenly I saw my dreams, my hope, my life forever fulfilled: my father stood in the doorway. This time, he was not smiling, but crying.

"I escaped," he said, again and again, embracing all of us. I know that I have no right to do so, but ever since that time, I have believed in miracles.

He was hungry. We went to the kitchen, but there was little food. We had not seen eggs for several weeks by then, and there had been no meat or cheese or milk for us for almost as long as that. But he ate some pea soup and enjoyed it very much, telling us about his escape. Marching for several days from Gödöllő westward, among hundreds dying on the way to the Austrian border, he had woken up from his sleep last night, he said, in a field crammed with Jews lying around him on the ground. Crawling through the place and the section where the tents of the guards stood, he dared to stand up and walk after a while. Then he tore the yellow star from his coat, reaching the train station in the nearest town after an hour or two, in the middle of the night. He went to a restroom and ripped the money out of the lining of his coat, where my mother had sewn it before he had left home, and bought a ticket to Budapest from a bearded, sleepy old man behind the counter. He boarded the train at 2:00 A.M. The journey had its own dangers: the train had halted at times for hours, waiting for other trains at certain stations, or, at times, in open fields. And it had been crowded with Hungarian and German soldiers. He hid his face in his coat, he said, and pretended to be asleep. Nobody had asked him for identification papers. Arriving in Budapest at the Western Station, which was for the moment—and by pure luck—free of police and the Nyilas rounding up Jews, he walked across the deserted streets, straight home.

"I felt I was holding your hands," he told us.

I fell asleep in his arms. Later, waking up, I played for him the last part of the first Beethoven piano sonata in f minor. Everybody cried.

"But we cannot risk staying here any longer," he said. "We need to leave at the latest tomorrow morning."

Erzsi left; she wanted to check out something, she said. I could not sleep all night, watching the threshold under the door of my parents' room. The stream of light flickered.

21

HOMELESS

Waking up next morning, we got dressed immediately and sat down to eat a piece of bread on which we spread cherry jam, my mother's last jar, which she had prepared the year before. A few minutes later Erzsi appeared, her lovely, heart-shaped face unrecognizably hard and strict.

"You must leave here immediately," she said. "The Nyilas are all over the street."

"But where are we going?" asked my mother desperately. "*In the street?*"

"Come on," said Erzsi, and she was crying. "At this moment nothing matters, just this: we must leave this house! And if we succeed, we won't stay in the street: I have the keys to the pharmacy belonging to the Funks."

The Funks were my father's best friends, from the time he was a student at the university. While they were Jews, a pharmacist son-in-law of theirs, Imre Nagy, was not. For the past few years, the pharmacy had been running under his name. This meant it was not "Jewish property." Hence, for us it could be a perfect shelter.

With trembling hands my mother cut off the yellow stars she had sewn on our coats a long time before.

We ran down the stairway. Nobody saw us. Our neighbors in the ghetto house either knew what was taking place in the streets and had now withdrawn into their apartments, getting ready for the evacuation, or were simply very careful. It was around 8:00 A.M. We arrived

130

downstairs; my father had an old key to the front door. He opened it. There was nobody on the stairs outside, nobody in the front yard, nobody outside the gate in front of the house, and nobody on the high school side of Abonyi Street. We crossed to the left. But looking down on Szent Domonkos Street toward Thököly Street, we saw a group of Nyilas standing. We changed our course to the right. Abonyi Street was empty. Walking with measured steps toward the next cross street, we turned left on Aréna Street, which took us to Thököly Street, where people were hurrying in all directions. We turned right and walked for a short while toward the East Station, till we arrived at the Funks' pharmacy. The place was closed down, big signs in its window, as there were in many other shop windows at this point: "Till further notice, this business is closed." Of course, there had been good reasons to close down all businesses in Budapest. It was the middle of November 1944; for the past ten days, the city had been nearly encircled by the Soviet troops. We could hear the roaring of guns and explosions, as well as the distant bombing of the suburbs of Budapest. We went inside the house and entered the pharmacy from the back.

Breathing deeply, we arrived. Then we sat down in the back room where, before, the pharmacist on call had slept. There was a large couch, a desk, and a wardrobe. I felt very comfortable there. In order to bring us food for the next few days, and perhaps even an assignment to one of the apartments under the protection of the Vatican, Erzsi left immediately. By the time she returned, it was 4:00 P.M. She showed us the papers she had stood five hours in line for: we were assigned to move into a large apartment house, 17 Aréna Street (on the corner of Abonyi Street), an apartment house that was under the protection of the Vatican.

"We are saved," sighed my father.

22

THE VATICAN HOUSE

We picked up our backpacks, which held food for two days and a change of underwear. Mine also had a nightgown, two blouses and two skirts, one pullover, a biography of Bach, and the last two volumes of *The Count of Monte Cristo* by Dumas. We left the Funk pharmacy before evening. I remember it was still light, but I was terrified on the street, crowded with people. Erzsi had her arm around me as we walked, following my father, mother, and Iván.

It must have been around 4:30 P.M. when we entered the Vatican house. Showing our papers to a man standing guard at the door, we entered the stairway. Erzsi went home. Our assigned apartment was located on the third floor. We rang the doorbell; somebody opened the door. The place was packed with large groups of the elderly, in addition to many younger men and women, and children. Several people were lying on the floor; others sat on the beds, on chairs, on sofas, everywhere. I saw bodies mingled with bodies; some looked as if they were lying on top of each other. There were no rooms among those we saw in the apartment that could accommodate even one more person. And we were a family of four! Standing in the middle of the entrance hall, while talking to a man calling himself "the manager of the apartment," my father offered him money if he would make space for us. The man pointed to a door that opened from the corridor. My father entered the place; I snuck behind him, and we found ourselves in a tiny "servant's room." It had but a wardrobe and one bed, in which, apparently, nobody slept. It was like heaven to us in comparison to the overcrowded rooms where people were lying on top of one another. Immediately my father signed the papers the "manager" had for him. For the next couple of hours I read. Later, we lay down. My father, my mother, and I slept in the bed, Iván, on the floor. We at least had a place to stay now.

I woke up early in the morning. Something tickled my mouth. Wiping it off, I turned to the other side. But again, I felt something like a cobweb across my face. I sat up in bed, rubbing it off. It was dark outside. In the room everybody was sleeping. I lay down and fell asleep. When I woke up next morning, it was light. My eyes met Iván's. He stood above me, on top of the bed, looking at me for a moment; then he tried to catch some thin, brown material hanging from the ceiling. It was waving in the air, as if blown by the wind.

"What is that?" I asked. "It hung into my bed and bothered me all night."

"You don't want to know," he said.

I stood up on my toes on the bed. It was some time before I understood what I saw. It was horrible. Nests of bedbugs hung from the ceiling on thin threads, embedded into one another. They appeared like a woven structure made of raisins and veils of dust. Thousands of bedbugs lived within them. It took Iván a long time to tear down the whole, uneven construction. This did not mean, of course, that we got rid of all the bedbugs. They never ceased sucking our blood while we lived in the "protected house of the Vatican." We scratched our bodies all the time, our skin covered with itchy bites. Still, however disgusting, they were significantly less dangerous than the lice that overran us later, in the bunker, at our last "refuge" on Kisfaludy Street, at the "White Cross Hospital."

Although there were many children in the Vatican house—I counted twenty-four just in the apartment where we lived—there was no time or space to establish relationships, to get to know someone, or even to play a few of the old games we used to play with our friends at Abonyi Street. I made friends with two adults in the Vatican house, an old woman who loved to read and a young one who was pregnant and loved music. Her husband was in the labor service. She, like all of us, was waiting impatiently for the end of the war, for the arrival of the Soviet troops in Budapest.

23

WITCHES' SHABBAT

But for that we had to wait for a long time. On December 3, 1944, in the Vatican house, we woke up again to the screams of the Nyilas, the gang of Hungarian National Socialists.

"Out of bed, lazy swines," the call echoed all over the house. "Men between sixteen and fifty, women between sixteen and forty-five, must gather downstairs in separate groups, the rest, in another, forming lines of five. Only the sick may stay. You must be there in ten minutes. One second late, and you'll be shot dead."

Our window opened directly on the corridor that curved around and led from the apartment where we lived to the staircase, while four flights underneath, a closed courtyard stretched across. We saw through the curtain the shadows of men running with rifles slung from their shoulders, but we did not dare draw the curtain: they would have noticed us immediately. We got dressed hastily. In the meantime, we heard the front doors' glass shatter and the men shouting and smashing objects throughout the apartment. We dared not move. Suddenly everything grew quiet. A minute later, a policeman entered our room; staring at us, he turned to my father:

"Take off your coat and let the children go," he said. "They will be taken to the ghetto. And that's OK for the moment; but get them out of there as soon as you can. As for now," and he pointed toward my father, "you should immediately go to bed. Say you are sick, and for the time being your wife will be allowed to stay with you as your caretaker." Then he disappeared.

To this day, we wonder who this man was. Several of our friends to whom we told the story after the war thought he might have belonged to one of the Zionist underground groups of young Jewish men who wore Arrow Cross or police uniforms and appeared in the chaos of the evacuation processes, even during the shootings in November and December 1944. They tried to pretend to be members of the police or the Nyilas. At the same time, they did everything to stop or at least slow down the ongoing atrocities. Or perhaps he was just a truly decent police officer, sick of the cruelties and destruction committed by the Arrow Cross.

At this moment, however, we had no time to evaluate his advice. We believed him and did what he said we should. Almost automatically, my father started to undress. I ran to him and my mother for a last embrace and left with Iván. Assembling on Aréna Street, we saw for the first time the large mass of people gathered in the Vatican house. I started to count them, but there were more and more coming, so that I lost track again and again. After a while, I gave up counting, but thought that there were several hundred people standing in line. Our guards were screaming constantly; and somewhat later, they started to shoot into the air. Then they had roll calls; if there was no answer from the group, they ran back into the house, trying to locate the missing person or persons. If I remember well, in the end, they found most of them. After hours of waiting, we were marched off. The sky was dark; it started to drizzle.

"Swines," one of the Nyilas boys shouted. "You won't live for five more minutes unless you move faster."

We tried to do so, marching toward Podmanicky Street. On our route from the Vatican house on Aréna Street to Dohány Street, we stopped in front of several houses. Some were under Swiss or Red Cross protection, others were under that of the Vatican or Sweden. In front of each of these houses we had to wait, at times for hours. But after the third or fourth building was "cleansed" of Jews, the Nyilas got tired and impatient, starting to fling their rifles about, even aiming at people assembled for the roll calls. Reading long lists of names, they ordered those whose names were not on the lists to stand in line and marched them off separately "for a good swim," as our guards informed us (which meant to be shot into the Danube). The rest were forced into endless lines and moved toward the ghetto. The ordeal showed no sign of ending. In fact, it became worse. After a while, our guards started to shoot people who seemed to cause "problems" in the group. One of them was an old lady who came from the apartment we had lived in.

"My daughter, my daughter," she cried during our march from the Vatican house, and repeated again and again, "They took her away; she'll never come back." I heard her sobbing for hours. Then I heard nothing; and after a while I forgot to pay attention to her crying. Shaken by what was taking place, fearing deportation and life without my parents, I started to feel that I was losing my strength. My knees trembled, my heart was racing, I did not want to go on. Then I started to have a discussion with Iván about what would happen to us without our parents.

"Don't worry," Iván said, pressing my hand. "I'll never leave you!" This gave me a new impulse to walk faster; although desperate, I suddenly had some strength to move on.

The ground was wet. Waiting in front of yet another "protected house," I suddenly noticed the old woman again. But now, she was crawling on all fours in the snow that had fallen during the afternoon.

"Ilonka," she cried, "Ilonka!"

"Get off your hands and stand on your feet, dirty old bitch," screamed a young man in an Arrow Cross uniform, "or I'll shoot you dead!"

Again she started scrambling on all fours: "Ilonka! Ilonka!"

Someone tried to lift her up. At this moment, I saw the boy aiming, and I heard two shots: *pop-pop.* By now the snowflakes had started to turn into sleet and rain. I stared at the red fluid that combined with the slush and filled up a hole in the ground. Something held me back from looking around me.

"Close your eyes," Iván screamed at me. But then I opened them and looked back. Behind me, I saw the old woman, white hair, dark coat, lying on the ground. Her eyes were open and so was her mouth. Blood gushed from her throat. Next to her, a man lay on his stomach; on his back, his coat was torn; a huge red stain grew ever larger on his shoulder. There was still some white snow around. But much of it was starting to turn red.

"My God!" I cried in the arms of a lady whom I had never seen in my life.

The crowd was driven by fear. Some eight or nine Nyilas were now around us and an ever-growing mass of people standing on the streets.

"We'll shoot you dead, right now!" two boys with rifles screamed.

We ran; I was out of breath.

The raid ended at night. By the time we arrived in the ghetto, it was pitch dark. Being pushed downstairs in a house somewhere near Dohány Street, we arrived at the basement. There was a multitude of people. A few sat on makeshift chairs, but most of them were on the ground, exhausted. Looking around, I recognized Mr. and Mrs. Mérő, our neighbors at 10 Abonyi Street and fellow residents in the Vatican house. Crying for a while with them, I fell asleep.

When I woke up next morning, I knew where I was; and I did not open my eyes. But then I heard Iván's voice, and I looked around surprised:

"How wonderful to see you, my friend! My God! How did you get here?"

I lay on the ground next to an elderly lady. But I just glanced at her. My gaze was concentrated on the middle-aged man Iván was talking to: brown-gray hair, brown-gray mustache, kind face. Who was he? I knew him; I knew him very well, but I did not know *who* he was.

"Your father sent me to you! He wants to know that you are well. Write your parents now; I will take your letters to them."

"Take our letters to them?" I thought. Of course, this was our mailman who came by every day when we lived on Abonyi Street. I had known him for all the years we lived there.

I no longer remember—or perhaps I never knew—how my father and Erzsi got hold of this kind-hearted man and convinced him to go inside the ghetto, looking for us amid the chaos of the comings and goings of the Arrow Cross gangs who were driving around large masses of Jews. At any rate, he came and brought us news from our parents, assuring us of their well-being. I sat down immediately to write a letter, telling them that we were well and that I hoped we could soon be together. Also the Mérős wrote a few lines, promising to take care of us.

The sweet, good mailman took our letters and came back with an answer within a few hours. I read and reread my father's note all day, feeling his presence, telling myself over and over that we would soon be together again. The messenger left, but not before he assured us that Erzsi would pick us up within the next few days. One day passed. I could think of nothing else but of her taking me back to my parents. I missed them so much! While Iván started to find some friends, I was lonely and terrified. And most people were. Even the Mérős cried constantly; they did not know where their children were.

Hoping for messages all the time, we were also very hungry, but there was not much to eat except the bean soup we were given every morning. Periodically, new transports of Jews arrived in the basement, where so many people lived right now that one could hardly move around anymore. I sat on the floor and waited.

Then I got tired of sitting in one place and decided to go for a walk. Moving along the streets, I suddenly noticed a muddy, wet newspaper trampled into the ground in front of a house in Dob Street. I bent down and picked it up. I had not seen a newspaper for weeks. It was the obituary page. I saw Faragó's name. Shaking, I tried to read the column. With his achievements described, it gave account of his life, illness, and death. I felt stabbed by pain. Sobbing and running back to the basement of the house where we now lived, I told Iván and those around me that I loved him and would never forget him for as long as I lived.

I am not sure how much time went by, two days or three, but one morning Erzsi arrived and walked away with us from the ghetto. I still do not quite understand how this happened. But what I do know is that she suddenly appeared in the basement, and while helping me put on my coat, she whispered into my ears that from now on I was Zsuzsanna Ákom and that I must not forget my name. I did not mind anything. The mere fact that she had come and that she knew where my parents were gave me back my strength.

On the corner of the next street, a military guardhouse stood with some Nyilas inside, blocking the road. They demanded birth certificates and registration papers from everybody leaving the ghetto.

Pointing to me and Iván, Erzsi took out all the papers from her handbag.

"These children are my relatives," she announced nonchalantly. "They had originally come from Békéscsaba. But with the front getting dangerously close to Csaba, their mother wanted them to leave town and flee from the Russians. I asked her to send them to Budapest. They have lived here ever since October. But now that this whole area is turning into a ghetto, I want them to leave and move to my apartment." (Békéscsaba had been in Soviet hands since October; hence, nobody could check our registration with the police.)

I trembled: Would they believe Erzsi? Would they tell Iván to drop his pants?

The Nyilas in the guardhouse took our papers and studied them; then, gesturing toward the guards at the gate, they called, "Let them go."

We left the ghetto.

We were free.

I was happy walking next to Erzsi and Iván on the streets of Budapest. It was cold, but we were free. I looked for people wearing the yellow star, but I saw none. There were many passersby on the street; some of them brushed against us, hurrying who knows where. Some were moving, pushing carts loaded with furniture. Others were carrying packages. But most of them were rushing, looking shaken and frightened. Small wonder. Being outside rather than hiding in the shelter of a building, one felt unprotected: if not the explosions of bombs, the crackle of gunfire racked the streets. The stores were closed in most neighborhoods, their windows broken. Much of the sidewalk was torn up, and many of the buildings we walked by had been destroyed by the ever-intensifying bombing. Their facades lay in ruins.

Luckily, we arrived at the Children's House of the Red Cross, where I would stay for the next several days. While two women registered us, Erzsi kissed me farewell and promised to return soon. I was taken to my room, where I met several girls. I tried to talk to them. But it did not help. I felt very lonely. I yearned for my parents. I did not know where they were, thinking sometimes that they might have been caught and murdered. What was going to happen to me? A three-year-old kissed my hand. I wanted to burst out laughing, but I could not. I cried. Looking for Iván, I went up the stairs. There he was, sitting around the table with several big boys. I listened to their discussions. But I could not get involved: they were talking about the resistance movement of the Yugoslav partisans.

Unexpectedly, a few days later, Erzsi appeared. She announced that she had to separate us from one another now since she had found a safe house for me, where I could remain till the end of the war. Iván, she explained, would have to go into hiding a bit later. She would return in a few days to pick him up and deliver him to the place he would stay. The safe house for me was a cloister on Nefelejts Street. The nuns, she told me, had taken in a number of refugee girls. There was a good chance, she added, that several of them are Jewish. But since I appear as Zsuzsanna Ákom in my papers, born as a Lutheran, I must not change my identity. In fact, I should remain Zsuzsanna Ákom and never tell anybody that I am Zsuzsanna Abonyi until the end of the war. Then, finally, I would be able to use my real name.

Kissing Iván farewell, I felt terribly sad. And when I went back to my room to gather my belongings, I thought of something that had never crossed my mind before: What if something happened and Erzsi could not come to see me anymore? I would die alone. I felt as though my heart had stopped beating. We walked silently from the Red Cross house to the convent. It was a long way. Erzsi kept her hands in her pockets. I knew they were trembling.

Again it was sleeting, and the streets were full of hurrying people. The background noise was unbearable and threatening. The thunder of artillery and constant explosions echoed around us. I was terribly frightened. Erzsi said that what we heard cracking nearby was rifle fire, and the blasts came from assault guns. She also told me over and over not to be afraid: rather think of the siege and its battles as necessary for our freedom. Yet at times, when the rattling and booming got close to us, she just grabbed my arm and dragged me into a house, running with me to the shelter. And people in these houses always let us in. When things quieted down, we ran out and walked on. The streets looked distorted by pain.

It was dark by the time we arrived at the convent. Two nuns were waiting for us on the staircase. Erzsi could not speak; neither could I. Nor did the nuns ask any questions. Silently Erzsi handed them my papers and left. They showed me to my room, which I was to share with three other girls. But the girls were sleeping already. I lay down on a bed already made for me and immediately fell asleep.

24

ALONE

Next morning, I opened my eyes and saw the girls standing near my bed, staring at me and laughing. Among them was a tall teenager with black curly hair, Erika; a small one, with big green eyes, Borika; and between them, a smiling redhead, Anna. They said they were glad to see me. But we did not have much time to chat. The two nuns taking me around the night before entered our room and urged us to hurry up. We did so. Taken to the dining room, I looked around and saw perhaps twenty-five to thirty girls, talking, standing, sitting, all together, among them little ones as well as teenagers. We too sat down at a small round table. Before we ate, however, we were told to bow our heads, fold our hands, and say prayers—none of which I had ever heard before.

Resonating in the room, our praying voices covered up the distant thunder of the cannons, but they could not cover up the rattling of machine guns quite nearby and the loud explosions.

"Api, Mami, please come and save me!" I cried inside; and my heart beat faster. I knew I must not show what I felt. "Oh God! Let us survive," I prayed silently; "and, please, let Erzsi come and take me away from here, and please, please, let me go back to my parents."

After praying, we were allowed to eat. Milk, bread, and margarine were on the table; despite the explosions, despite my fears, I was very hungry, wolfing down everything I saw.

After lunch, some children carried the dirty dishes to the kitchen, while the rest sat quietly. Then everybody was given a string of beads, the likes of which I had never seen before. It consisted of many sections, separated from one another by a larger bead, with its two ends joining a string holding a cross. I did not know what this chaplet was; when I asked, one of the girls told me: "A rosary." We then had to recite a very long prayer, which I learned by heart during that first morning, because we said it over and over until noon. As we stopped, at times for just a second, we heard the roar of the cannons come closer, and I became increasingly fearful of the constant explosions. We prayed until lunch. But as soon as we finished eating, all the nuns gathered around us again, and we said the rosary throughout the afternoon as well.

I wanted to talk to somebody, somebody who knew me, who knew us, somebody I could tell about my father: how good and how handsome he was, and how beautifully he played the viola and the cello. And what beautiful shades of blond my mother's hair had, how mellow her voice was, and what impact her lyrical intensity had on me when I accompanied her performance of Schubert songs. But nobody seemed interested. Supper ended very fast, and we were rushed to go to sleep.

Finally, in bed, the four of us tried to talk, to laugh a bit, to get acquainted with one another. But the nuns came in, at first to wish us a good night, but later to check whether or not we were still chatting. And when they heard us laughing and talking, they got very angry. Still, we continued to whisper under the blankets, talking about the siege, the explosions, the bombs. After a while, the girls spoke of their parents and siblings, each claiming that as soon as the war came to an end, their families would pick them up and take them home. Home? Where was that? I did not even know the names of the towns they mentioned. And where were their parents now? And where were mine? I dared not cry. I told them mine lived in the countryside. And soon, I fell asleep.

Waking up next morning, we had to hurry to get ready and take our seats in the dining room, just as we had the day before. In fact, it did not take long to note that there was no difference between the events of the first day of my arrival in the convent and the second, no difference in the schedules of these two days or the rest of my stay in that place. We always had to hurry to get up, to wash, and eat breakfast; and having done so, we started to pray, continuing to pray from morning till noon; and then again, after lunch, during the afternoon till supper. Sometimes we stopped for a short while and read questions and answers out of a catechism given to us—some of which we even briefly discussed. But we were not allowed to spend a long time discussing these questions. As soon as possible, we went back to praying. I could only converse with the girls at night, and only for a short while. The nuns constantly checked the rooms, making sure that everybody was asleep. I felt oppressed by their control and by the weight of this monotonous existence. I was dying to talk to someone; at the same time, I was desperately homesick for my parents. I longed for their voices, for their kisses, for their embrace. I also feared that the Nyilas would come one day to the convent, looking for me, and take me away. How would my father live if they killed me?

Then, one day, in the morning, after a long stream of "Hail Mary's," I stood up and went to the toilet. As I entered, I met Erika, my roommate. Nobody was in the corridor. We fell into each other's arms and quickly withdrew to the bathroom, locking the door. Finally, we were alone; and we could talk without "the little ones"—and without the nuns around us. Looking into Erika's eyes, I had a strange feeling: Could she be Jewish?

She bent over the sink, washing her face: "My mother!" she cried, "Where is my mother?"

I needed to hear no more: "And where is mine?" I asked sobbing and embraced her. Then I continued: "Are you Jewish?"

She looked at me with great amazement. "No," she said. "Are you?"

"Yes I am," I answered. "I was smuggled out of the ghetto by Erzsi, who brought me here." Tremendously relieved, I sighed: it was out in the open. At least Erika knows now who I am, I thought, and was happy. She said something but I do not remember what. We returned to the group of children we had left. Their heads bent, they were praying. We joined them.

It happened in the late afternoon, just before we finished praying in the large room, that a nun came in to look for me and pick me up from the dining room.

"Let's go to your bedroom," she said softly. "You need to find your backpack and gather your things."

"Me? Why? Alone?" I asked. We were walking down the corridor.

"Erzsi is here to take you away!"

I could not breathe. "Has something happened to my parents?" I asked.

"No, no," she said, and was smiling, "but you need to go!"

I met Erzsi under the staircase. Several nuns were standing around her.

"Bye-bye," they called and waved to us. "Good luck to both of you."

"What happened?" I asked Erzsi, as soon as we were outside, kissing her hands and face, overwhelmed by the cold, but dancing and jumping up and down. I felt liberated, greatly relieved, and happy; but I was also dizzy from my rapid release.

"I have no idea," she said. "I took some food to your parents, and when I got home, there was a note from one of the tenants on the second floor that said I should call the convent." (Wanting to talk to Erzsi, callers had to leave their message with her neighbors, who were kind enough to take it.) "I did, and then the nun I spoke with told me to visit the convent no matter how late I came home tonight. And if it were too late, it must be tomorrow morning at 7:15 A.M., whenever the law permits it. So I came just now."

"And?" I asked.

"Well, I arrived," she said. "They received me in the office. One of them spoke. She said you told one of your roommates that you were Jewish, giving out information that should never have become public. Now that it has, you have become a threat to the convent, to the rest of the children, and to yourself. The nuns said, if the Arrow Cross wanted to search the convent, they could easily figure out who you were. Or if some of the convent's employees ever heard about 'the story' you had told your roommate, and denounced the nuns for hiding you, the place would be closed down. The rest of the children would have to leave. And the nuns themselves would be hurt. 'Therefore,' they agreed, 'Zsuzsi must leave here immediately!'"

"Good," I said, and was quite relieved. "I didn't like it there!"

"It's not good," Erzsi said desperately, "it's bad! What are we going to do now? We are standing on the street. It is 4:30 P.M.; soon it will be dark, and we are not permitted to be on the street after 5:00 P.M."

"And Api?" I asked and cried, and suddenly felt enormously guilty, "and Mami? Are they alive?"

"They are," she said, "but we won't be for long if we stand here. Let's go somewhere."

We started out walking, listening to the constantly pounding artillery in the background.

Erzsi took me to her cousin Irma, offering her one of my mother's golden bracelets. I could stay there for the night, Irma agreed, but Erzsi should pick me up in the morning because, Irma insisted, with the bombing and cannon fire getting worse, she would like to move to a shelter, just as most people of the house had already done, rather than stay in the apartment. And, of course, I must not follow her there because she could not explain to the others who I was, and she would not want to "get into trouble." Erzsi swore she would pick me up the next day. She left; I sat down on a kitchen chair, where I remained seated throughout the night.

Erzsi returned the next day around noon. She had found a place for me, she said, in an apartment house on the banks of the Danube. I would be looked after by a young woman by the name of Mrs. Lóránt. We waved farewell to Irma and started out immediately, walking across Budapest.

Probably ten to twelve days had passed since our last journey from the Children's Red Cross Home to the convent. It is true that the night before we had walked from the convent to Irma's. But it had been late, and dark clouds hung over Budapest. It had been raining. I had not seen anything. The streets and the horizon had been covered by a wintry mix of hurrying people and darkness. Now I could not believe what I saw. The plaster was gone from most of the houses, many of which were completely destroyed, while others had huge and small parts torn from their structures that lay in the rubble. The plaster dust in the streets made breathing difficult. With smoke and flames covering the horizon, we heard the noise of heavy gun battles. At times, shells exploded close to us, shattering windows and creating further smoke and flames. Erzsi's face was hard, and she forced me to hurry. Crowds of people were on the street, but when the detonations came close, they all ran into the nearest building, as did we. Sometimes we ran as far as the shelter. In many cases, however, we could not go inside because the basements were already full of people who had moved out of their apartments and settled in the bunkers. Staying in the staircase for a while, we came out when the bombs and the guns moved elsewhere. Then we continued on our way. We had to interrupt our walk several times, however, before we arrived at our goal: a house of several stories on the bank of the Danube.

By then the horizon was wrapped in a mournful light, just before nightfall. We went up four flights of stairs. A tall, thin, beautiful young lady opened the door. Two suitcases stood in the entrance hall.

"I am prepared for everything in case we have to move to the bunker," she said.

"Well," said Erzsi slowly, "I am not sure that Zsuzsi should go there."

"Let's see how things develop. We won't do that unless it's necessary," said the kind lady.

"OK, but try to avoid it; and if you have to go, please take care of Zsuzsi," said Erzsi. "Say you are her aunt."

"I shall," she smiled.

Erzsi reached inside the pocket of her winter coat. She gave the woman my mother's last golden bracelet, decorated with sapphire. The lady smiled and embraced me, taking us to my room, showing me the kitchen and the bathroom of her apartment. I was happy and frightened at the same time.

"How long will I have to be here?" I asked Erzsi when we were left alone for a minute.

"I don't know," she said. "Perhaps until the Russians come, who, as you can see and hear, are already very close; or perhaps until I can find a place for you together with your parents."

"Oh my God," I thought, "how will I survive?"

The lady returned.

"Take care of her," Erzsi said. "I'll be here to visit you within a few days."

She embraced me and left.

"Just ask me about anything you need." The young lady stroked my hair.

"I will," I said, and went to my room. Lying down, I fell asleep immediately.

25

THE SIEGE

I slept until the morning, when explosions started to shake the room. The front windows of the house opened to the Danube: they were exposed to the barrage. Within seconds the concussions and shrapnel from the artillery and mortar rounds pounded the blinds, shattered the glass, and broke every piece of furniture in the room, knocking off the lamp, blowing holes into the walls, turning much of the place into rubble. Frightened to death, I first hid under the blanket, then jumped out of bed and yanked the door open.

"Mrs. Lóránt," I screamed, "let's leave!"

Of course, deep down, I knew that we could not leave. Erzsi had told me so. It would be dangerous to go to the shelter, even if I were taken by Mrs. Lóránt, she warned me, because people gathered there would immediately notice that I was a stranger. Some might even think that I was a Jewish child hiding from the authorities and decide to call the police.

"Of course, your story as a refugee from Békéscsaba," she had argued and tried to reassure me and, I think, herself, "is quite believable. Your papers are proper, and your status not at all unusual—after all, Budapest has been overrun by refugees, and among them are many children. Still, being noticed, you might be exposed to danger, or at least to intense interrogations. Therefore, it is better," Erzsi had concluded, "to avoid such confrontation."

Amid the rise of dust inside the room and the roar of guns outside, however, I forgot about these warnings. I simply was looking for the beautiful landlady who had been so kind to me the previous night. I wanted to talk to her, share with her my fear; to have contact with a human being, rely on an adult, who would know, and could tell me, what to do. But in vain did I look for her; in vain did I call her name. I could not find her. With the shooting sometimes far off, sometimes quite nearby, I searched desperately for her, running through every room again and again. I started to tear open all the doors of the apartment, looking under the beds, into the closets, into the bathroom. Still I did not find her.

Driven by panic, I kept calling out again and again, "Mrs. Lóránt, where are you?"

No answer. After a long silence, the thunder from the shooting resumed. Running to an entrance hall that had no windows, except two small ones opening to the corridor, I yanked open one of three doors and discovered a large closet in a very small room. Jumping in, I saw on the shelves, and threw on the floor, a pile of bed sheets and pillowcases. In addition, I looked around and noticed blankets and summer clothes as well as several pairs of sandals. The place felt comfortable; if I closed the door, even the explosions were muffled. I made myself a seat on the floor.

Suddenly I could hear the rattle of machine guns get louder; this was followed by an eerie silence. I crawled out of the closet. Still looking for Mrs. Lóránt, I searched the apartment and went to the bathroom. It was clean, in fact, immaculate. Opening the cabinets, I noticed that they held no toothbrush, no toothpaste, no hairbrush, no soap, no perfume. The shelves were empty. Fear grabbed my insides. I suddenly remembered that I had looked around that bathroom the night before and admired Mrs. Lóránt's pink toothbrush and her lipsticks placed around the sink. Now I could see none of them, either around the sink or in the cabinets.

"She isn't here at all," I thought.

Everything was quiet outside. I ripped her closet doors open; it was empty.

"Did she leave?" I screamed to myself. "Where did she go? And why?"

Looking into the large closet for a while, I suddenly thought, "My God! I am alone!"

And I was. (Mrs. Lóránt had left the apartment with her German boyfriend on the night of my arrival, taking along, of course, my mother's bracelet and everything else that was portable, including every bit of food.) Not knowing this at the time, I just stood in the middle of the apartment, with my feet rooted to the ground. Unable to locate her and quite undecided about what to do, I returned to my room. Only then did I notice that the place had been completely devastated by the morning's attack.

The street was silent. Then suddenly the chorus of guns started anew. I took refuge inside the closet. It took me a while to note, though, that these explosions were different from those before. Now it was not the house that was under fire but something else, I thought. Indeed, the shots came directly from the street. Or perhaps from the river? I crawled on all fours. Arriving at the window with its broken panes, I tried to look outside through the shattered blinds. But what did I see? My God! It was an image I will not forget for as long as I live: a bunch of children, men, and women were standing on the bank of the Danube, on their chests the palm-sized yellow star. They were bound together by ropes. At least four or five Nyilas aimed their guns at them, shooting them into the river, which flowed red like blood. Nobody screamed; nobody cried. You could hear nothing but the shots and the splash of the bodies falling into the red foam. In panic, I threw myself on the floor. The marketplace where Hanna's father and grandfather were murdered appeared before my eyes.

"All of us will be shot," I thought. Then I must have lost consciousness because I remember nothing further. My first memory of the morning after the shooting floats around my attempts to get up from the floor. At this point, I could think of nothing other than leaving the apartment and running away. But where to?

In the corridor, cold air hit my face. That slowed me down. And then, again, the front of the house was being pounded by shots. My hair stood on end. By now I had forgotten everything. All I knew was to run down the stairs. But there was a problem: the staircase had windows. In most of them, the glass had already been shattered by the shooting and explosions, although I think some still had panes because, as my father later discovered, a piece of splintered glass hit my knee. This hurt me. Amid the explosions, I kept on running. At this moment, gunshots started to pepper the walls of the staircase. I screamed and turned back, running up the stairs. Throughout my life, I have never ceased to wonder about these incomprehensible moments during which I was running first down, then up the stairs, between the first and the fourth floor of that staircase pelted by bullets, in the house that stood on the banks of the Danube River, where I stayed alive. Then the rattle of the guns subsided. Bombs fell instead. By the time I arrived at the fourth floor, I saw from the corridor flames and black smoke rising from several houses in the street. My heart beating, I went inside the apartment. Complete silence followed the bombardment. At this point, I remembered Erzsi's warning; I was happy about not making it to the shelter.

But I was enormously hungry. Searching for food in the kitchen and the pantry, I found, besides some ground poppies and pickled cucumbers, one large package of cookies that had fallen behind a broken shelf. I knew I must eat them as slowly as possible, so that they would last, as I told myself, "until the end of the war."

Trembling for a while and crying, I decided to "practice the piano in my head." I went back to the closet and started to imagine I was playing Beethoven's f-minor sonata, op. 3, from the first measure to the last. Some passages went very well, some, not at all. While my right hand's fingers were really singing in the second part, my left hand's were too slow playing the triplets in the fourth part.

"I need to practice this more," I thought. But I did not go back to "work" on those passages; rather, I started to play the second sonata in A major; and again, I thought through every single note. In the meantime, the bombing started anew.

"My poor father," I thought, "what will he do if I die? And my mother? Both of them would die!" I felt lonely and frightened in the closet and started to pray. I thought I would be closer to God if I prayed in Hebrew. But I knew very little Hebrew, so I mixed my personal prayer in Hungarian with such Hebrew prayers as the "Shema" and the Passover questions I had recited at our family's Seder in my grandfather's house back in the spring of 1940: "*Manishtana halylo ha zeh . . .*"

Praying for some time, I imagined again playing the piano: but this time, they were Bach fugues I practiced. And after a while, I think, I fell asleep.

I lived for three days in the closet, practicing pieces I played on the piano and knew by heart, acting out roles, real and imaginary ones alike. Also, I changed the roles of characters in a variety of plays, and recited poetry (my mother always wanted me to learn poems by heart), and I prayed and prayed and prayed. And while I believed I ate very little, as the time passed, I realized that I would soon be eating the last bites of my cookies. When that day arrived, I got truly frightened. Falling asleep, I woke up during the afternoon. It was then that I thought I could not stand it any longer: even if I died, I had to leave here. Putting on my coat, I stepped outside. Again the thunder of guns was loud, but then the noise subsided for a while. The air smelled like smoke. The house was quiet: I had no doubt that no one lived in these bombed-out apartments anymore, except me. Were people in the shelter or had they moved away? I leaned against the railing and looked down into the courtyard.

"What are you doing here, little girl? And where are your parents?" a kind voice asked me. Turning back, I saw a man about as old as my father, even faintly reminding me of him.

"I . . ." Here I stopped; sobbing tightened my throat. I could not continue the sentence. This man was the first person to talk to me in three or four days.

He looked at me. "Do you want to drink tea with us?"

I used to drink tea with my mother. Nobody else had ever asked me this question before.

"Yes," I said and cried.

"Come in," he waved, and pointed to the door next to the kitchen of the apartment where I lived.

The windows of this kitchen were covered by black cloth. Around a table sat two women: a young and beautiful one, with large brown eyes and curly brown hair—Vera, an eighteen-year-old girl—and an older one, with gray hair—her mother. I felt at home with them. The tea had a familiar dark, red-brown color, and it had an aroma out of heaven. The Szántó family had cube sugar as well, bread with butter, and a hard-boiled egg for everyone. I have never had anything taste better in my life. I sobbed while I ate. Of course they knew who I was. They, too, were Jewish; they, too, were hiding. In fact, Vera had fled from a group of women sent off on a death march. I told them about my parents, Iván, and Erzsi, and we talked and talked and talked. They invited me to stay with them, first of all because they thought that I should not be all alone in Mrs. Lóránt's apartment; second, because they thought that with the window panes shattered, a freezing wind would be blowing through that place. It was terribly cold there, they claimed, while they had a tiny gas heater in the kitchen that was still functioning. But I did not want to move. I explained to them that I was waiting for Erzsi, who would come and take me to my parents; and if she did not find me, she would think I had died. They argued that she would not come at night. She would be shot on the street if she tried. But I went back to sleep in the closet. And just as in a fairy tale, by the time I woke up next morning, I heard Erzsi's voice, calling, "Zsuzsika, where are you? I have come to pick you up." She was there.

Saying farewell to the Szántós, we had just began to walk down the stairs when the bombing started again. Erzsi took my hand and dashed with me down the stairs, through the doors and corridors to the basement. There she located the caretaker, who, as she told me later, had let her enter through the gate.

"Here is my little niece," Erzsi laughed happily, "the one I was talking to you about. As soon as the bombing stops, I'll leave with her, if this is OK?"

"Of course it is," said the woman, obviously concerned with other things.

Erzsi and I sat in the shelter for a while. Looking around, I noted that it was divided into several parts. In the section where we now sat, scores of people were sitting in chairs or lying on makeshift beds. But many of them lay on the floor on pillows or just on the ground. Some were praying. I think it was a kerosene lantern that flickered in the dark. Erzsi held me in her two arms. The constant explosions kept us breathless.

"Don't be afraid," Erzsi whispered in my ears, "the more they bomb, the sooner we'll be free!"

I knew that; and I was not afraid now.

"I don't mind dying," I told her, "but I don't want to die alone! Please, God," I begged, "let me find my parents."

It was exactly twenty days ago that we had parted.

26

WALKING ACROSS
THE UNDERWORLD

Later, when the air raid stopped, the two of us left. As soon as possible, we turned right from the street parallel to the Danube into a side street, leaving behind the road running alongside the banks of the river. Out of breath, we hurried as much we could, meeting on our way just a very few civilians; some of them were in horse-driven carts, some were running in the streets. The shelling was constant. Obviously, only those driven by hunger or the search for necessities were on the streets right now. The rest hid in the shelters. For good reasons. The city was engaged in one of the longest and bloodiest European battles of the Second World War, comparable in scale to those of Warsaw and Berlin. More than 160,000 people died in the bombing, shelling, and fighting, including 38,000 civilians.

As we walked across St. Stephen Boulevard, leaving behind the Western Station and subsequently the crossings of Andrássy, Rákóczy, and Üllői Streets, we arrived at the Kálvin Plaza. Throughout this long walk, we were again and again exposed to gunfire and bombing, with mortars hitting the houses around us, breaking the windows of the shops and the apartments we walked by, so that glass was crunching constantly under our feet. We hurried along the streets rather than the sidewalks, hiding sometimes under the gates of houses or staircases, or behind trees and poles. At times we met soldiers, saw Germans in tanks, and were screamed at by the Nyilas, who were driving along groups of

Jews. We also saw civilians running down the sidewalks, their faces distorted by fear. Twice we had to stop on our way and beg strangers to allow us to use their shelters till the bomb attacks subsided.

It was after 4:00 P.M. when we arrived at the "White Cross Hospital" on Kisfaludy Street. Entering through the gate, I saw my father from afar. He stood next to the inside door, watching the street. I ran into his arms. He had lost much weight. His face had aged tremendously, becoming much smaller than before. With dark moons under his eyes, he looked tortured. Both of us were crying. Erzsi was crying as well, but after hugging us, she said she did not want to come inside. She had to hurry to get home to Iván, who was living with her, hiding in our former apartment. We said farewell to one another, because we knew she would have a long walk to Abonyi Street (almost as long as we had walked from the banks of the Danube to Kisfaludy Street). She left. When she turned back to wave, we saw her smile but also the tears running down her face.

My father held me in his arms; he took me to my mother. She was sobbing and could not stop sobbing through the night.

27

THE "WHITE CROSS HOSPITAL"

Our asylum for the next twenty-four days, the makeshift "White Cross Hospital" on Kisfaludy Street, claimed to be a branch of the highly reputable White Cross Hospital nearby, which had specialized in the health and welfare of children since the late nineteenth century. The place on Kisfaludy Street maintained that it was a branch of this organization and that it provided medical care for families in need of health care. But it did not. In reality, the "White Cross Hospital" on Kisfaludy Street was established with the help of a few Jewish physicians, some members of the Budapest Jewish Council, and a few young Zionists, all of whom were part of this rescue operation. Several of them dressed up and acted as the Nyilas, among the real Nyilas, with the latter screaming at us and ordering us around. Of course, all the "patients" were paying ransom, some of which the Nyilas kept for themselves, while they passed on the rest of the money to people high up in the city's administration. Functioning in the space of a former carpentry workshop, this "hospital" was one of those few establishments in Hungary that hid Jews during the period of December 1944 to January 1945. When the Soviet forces liberated Pest in 1945, most of the "hospital's patients" were still alive.

There were perhaps three or four doctors for about 120 to 150 "patients" in the "hospital"; three or four "nurses"; and about four or five Nyilas "guarding the place." The relatively large space of the former workshop held about thirty to forty two-tiered bunk beds (with four people in each unit). These units had nails hammered onto their "back wall," on which the "patients" would hang their coats, while keeping their personal belongings in bags on the beds. Behind the "back wall" of the bunk beds, straw sacks were thrown on the floor for people who wanted to sit up rather than lie down. Above these straw sacks were the windows of the workshop, covering the entire west side of the building. When I got there, on December 23, 1944, all the window panes were still in place.

It was wonderful to be with my parents. "As long as we are together," I said over and over, "nothing horrible can happen to us."

Feeling more secure, I started to look around for children my age. But I soon saw that there was not much opportunity for me to make friends in this place. First of all, there were no girls my age; nor did I see any boys to whom I wanted to talk. Not even the adults seemed to be open for discussions as they had been during the summer in the ghetto house, where I met several people who became my friends for the rest of my life. Later, I understood why! Here, most "patients" lacked any privacy or comfort. They were suffering enormously from the indignities of communal life and lived under constant threat to their existence. Reduced to their own devices, they were in no mood to tell, or listen to, stories, invent plays, or make friends.

And then there was something else that started to add fear and great discomfort to everyone's existence in the "hospital," undermining people's spirit and will to live: the lack of food, in fact, the terrible hunger with which we lived. Indeed, restricted ever since the late fall of 1944, food was now available for us only once a day. And the plateful of watery bean soup or lentils, prepared by "the personnel" in the kitchen, contained, as my father said, perhaps two hundred calories. Unless people had some biscuits or chocolate from the past in their backpacks or could buy some on the black market, which was becoming ever more limited because of the bombing, they started to starve. We had had a number of chocolate bars when my mother prepared our backpacks, before we went to the Vatican house. But when Iván and I were taken to the ghetto, my parents gave us their last ones. Succeeding in buying one or two more bars, my father had only one left in the last week of December. I ate that bar, while my parents found all kinds of excuses why they did not want to taste it. By then we, too, had started to starve. In addition, like everybody else, we were overrun by lice. Scratching the skin all over my body until it bled, I was covered with wounds.

The days passed. On the last day of December I sat, as always, on a big straw sack under the window and read. Immersed in a biography of the legendary, mad Russian dancer Nijinsky, who had married the daughter of the Hungarian actress Emilia Markus, I remember, I just had finished a chapter in the book, turning the page, when suddenly I saw the silver-blue, diamond flash of a completely unreal, enormously large, powerful, and cruel lightning bolt. It was sudden and frightening. Instinctively, as if jumping into a pond, I threw myself forward, grabbing every winter coat around me. They had hung on the "back wall" of the bunk beds, and I yanked them over my head and body. This saved my life, for the bomb made a direct hit. Some four or five people died in this moment, and there were several others who were wounded while sitting or walking under the glass windows that exploded when the bomb fell into the courtyard of the "hospital."

All the lights went out. The shards of the panes came raining into the room; some beds broke. The explosion was followed by silence for a short while. But then people started to scream names, probably those of their loved ones, while also trying to run outside the ward.

I climbed out from under the coats, crying desperately, "Mami, Api!"

The terrible smell of smoke settled in the place, while plaster fell everywhere. I stood amid masses of people who seemed to be stuck at the exit, but I too wanted to get out of there.

Then suddenly, I heard my mother's voice: "There she is! My God! She is bleeding!"

Indeed, blood poured from my mouth and nose, probably because of a concussion from the explosion; also, as I learned later, a piece of glass went into and was stuck in my chin. My mother took me in her arms, but we did not see my father for quite a while, not until the whirl of the large mass of people became a bit less chaotic and he found us in the crowd. Slipping and stumbling down the stairs, we descended with the rest of the people into the courtyard, where two corpses lay and some of the wounded were crying. And from there we moved through further corridors, down to a dark space, with its windows two feet above the ground, staring blindly into the air. My mother with some other women immediately started to cover the bodies with cloths. Soon my father left, and when he returned he was dragging some straw sacks along, which he put on the ground. We would sleep on them for the next seventeen days, until we were liberated by the Russians.

28

GOING HOME

The bombing was continuous. The buzzing of the airplanes never stopped, nor did the constant explosions.

"Come under my coat," I screamed at my parents when I heard that buzz. I became convinced, and it was their opinion too, that I had survived the blast that morning because of the coats I had pulled over my head and body. From now on, I believed that this was the only way to survive in the basement as well. Just to calm me down, I think, my mother hid with me under the blankets during the bombing most of the time. But my father was not always willing to do so. When he did, however, I was relieved. Although shaken by the blasts, crying, and pressing his hand, I felt better when he was there. Pulling our coats and blankets over our heads, he would sometimes lie with me for hours, telling stories from his childhood, which I loved to listen to. He spoke of Pali and Lulu, their father and mother, and the life they lived in Temesvár (but he rarely spoke of Bandi, the older brother, whom he adored and who had committed suicide). He also told me about the chamber music they played at home, and about the pieces he would like to play with me, about the pieces he loved, and about the pieces we would perform as soon as we went home. In fact, he promised me in the shelter on Kisfaludy Street that we would have weekly sessions of chamber music—not yet knowing that Lulu as well as Pali had been killed in the Holocaust and that, woefully missing them, he would be unable to play music for many years. In addition, he told me about his life during World War I, when he fought on the front as an eighteen-year-old and had been badly wounded. Then he prayed with me to his mother, who, he said, saved him when he had been shot in the head in that war and had lain unconscious on the ground for almost an hour. Found by his comrades, he was taken immediately to the rear lines, and from there to a hospital. And she saved him again, he said, when he had his head surgery to remove a bullet from a place near his brain, an operation in which most people usually died.

Now again, he prayed aloud to her, to help us, to save us, to let us live again. And he also promised me repeatedly, that one day we would get out of this basement, away from this nightmare, and "we'll live as human beings must, with our heads held up high rather than lowered."

Poor Father! I have been able to live my life as a free person; but he? Never.

For the moment, however, I was consumed by the fear of the ongoing bombardment. Ever since the moment of that brutal lightning, I shuddered whenever the bombs fell. Yet there was no doubt that I was better off than before, when I had been alone. I knew that. But Iván lived still apart from us, and this was the cause of my parents' constant worry. Indeed, they could not find a solution to the problem at this point of the siege. Because of the constant shelling and bombing of the city, people were not permitted to walk on the streets. Nor were private vehicles allowed on the roads. In short, my parents did not know how to get Iván away from the house on Abonyi Street. Nor could they, of course, communicate with him or with Erzsi. Yet they spoke of him constantly. They were terribly worried about the hostile environment he would suddenly have to face if the apartment became uninhabitable and he would be forced to move to the shelter, as we were now on Kisfaludy Street. He would obviously be recognized by some of the tenants of the apartment house, who, in turn, might denounce him to the police, while in the "White Cross Hospital," everybody was Jewish and everybody was hiding, including "the leadership" and "our guards." After hours of consideration, my father decided that despite all the weighty counterarguments, he would bribe and send one of the real "Nyilas," who acted as if they were guarding our hospital, but were really waiting for the end of the war, to pick Iván up and bring him to us.

He made this decision on the morning of January 2, 1945, two days after we moved to the shelter. He was just in the process of arranging things at some time in the early afternoon, when suddenly there was a commotion outside. A few minutes later, some of the "Nyilas" brought in Iván and Erzsi. With their faces and hands frostbitten, their winter coats filthy, they seemed quite happy, although very tired. They told us that they had been walking, at times crawling on all fours, or lying in the snow and mud. At other times, they just ran down into the shelters of nearby houses when the bombs were exploding. In the end, they survived, made it through the bombing, the explosions, and the Nyilas on the streets, and were now with us. Hugging me and crying, Erzsi said she did not want to leave right now. But my father thought it dangerous to stay.

"In case of a raid," he said, "they would take you together with us."

"And what do you think?" she asked. "Where would I want to go?"

That night she slept next to me on the straw sack. But next morning, my parents forced her to leave.

The days that followed were just like a bad dream. I screamed most of the time, becoming more and more desperate about the bombing. By now the workshop upstairs was a huge heap of rubble, and so was a big part of the shelter where we were. The house to the right of us was bombed out and so was the one on the left. I crawled under the blankets most of the time, still crying and begging my parents to come. Iván was different. He laughed at me and my blankets. He got up early every morning, and, unlike other people in the shelter, went outside before the bombing started and washed himself in the snow. He also spoke to me about the partisans in Yugoslavia, who were fighting against the Germans rather than hiding from them. Sometimes he played with me, and I loved that, especially when the explosions resounded from a distance. At times we played fantasy games and acted out roles, not so different from those we used to play during the summer back home. Most of the time, I had to play a little Jewish girl who was on the run from the Germans, whose brother joined the partisans and saved her in the end. These games were periodically interrupted by another one we often played—especially at night before falling asleep. It consisted of imagining different kinds of foods:

"*Ppopppy*seed cake," I said popping the consonants in the word.

"Cheesecake," he said, stretching the vowels as much as he could.

"Apple pie," I answered, "with lemon zest and cinna*mmmmmon*."

"Hmmm," he said thoughtfully. "Sachertorte," and he made a funny face, "big and dark brown, filled with STRAWBERRY preserves!"

"Cherry strudel," I said, unable to continue. The game made me desperately hungry.

The days passed; the bombing would not stop. One night we heard the Russian loudspeakers announcing, in Hungarian, the news. Some people living in the shelter went out, and when they returned, they told us what they had heard: Eastern Hungary had been occupied by the Red Army; Budapest was surrounded, and Soviet troops had taken much of Western Hungary as well. The Red Army leaders were calling on the people of Budapest to surrender.

"Just a few more days," said my father, "just a few more days."

But the German and Hungarian armies still resisted. In fact, I overheard a conversation between my father and a well-informed visitor from the other end of the shelter, who said that "our Nyilas" told him about the violent plans circulating among their "comrades," involving the killing of all Jews still alive in Budapest. Next to Hanna's marketplace, I recognized now the horrific image: the group of people I once saw standing on the banks of the Danube.

"Dear God! Don't let it happen," I sobbed and prayed. Between bombing and praying, the days passed by slowly. Shaken by the explosions, I lay on the ground, insane with fear, pressing the hands of my mother and father.

Then one day, in the morning, after a long air raid, the explosions stopped. An unusually long silence followed.

Then someone screamed, "The Russians."

And there they came: twelve big men, twelve angels, twelve times bringing life to us, shuffling down the stairs. Dressed in uniforms the likes of which I had never seen before, they were asking us whether or not there were any German soldiers on the premises: *"Nemetskiy soldat?"*

Many people kissed them; I did not. I was afraid. But I knew that they were our redeemers. Some of the survivors tried to talk to them in some international language, some showed them the yellow stars sewn on our overcoats, but the soldiers did not seem to be interested. They checked the premises, searched most people, making them give up their watches. Not mine, though. I had it on my arm, under my coat. Then they left. The shelter was in great confusion. Some people decided to leave immediately, some went out to look around the streets, others thought to stay for a while until we had more information about the status of the siege in the rest of the city. But it was clear that the bombing in Pest was over. We thought that the roar of guns as well as huge explosions could be heard only from Buda (still, there were some isolated battles going on for one more day in Pest).

"Pest is in Russian hands," called the loudspeakers everywhere. By then it was late morning, and everybody believed that we were free.

Iván wanted to leave. "It makes no sense to stay," he argued. "What is it that we would want to wait here for?"

My parents agreed. We gathered our things and left the shelter. Tearing off the yellow stars from our coats as we walked, we threw them on the half-frozen, muddy ground, next to the rest of the garbage (except for my mother, who put hers into her pocket). We started walking homeward.

On Kisfaludy Street and in its neighborhood, everything lay in ruins. In the streets and between the demolished houses, corpses lay scattered everywhere. We saw several burned-out tanks and groups of Soviet soldiers. Here and there, people were hurrying on the street. Then suddenly, we were stopped by two Russians. They stood on the street corner and demanded that we hand over our backpacks. We were amazed;

we did not know why. We had virtually nothing in them anymore. But searching the backpacks, they took out the two cans of sardines Iván had received as a gift before he came to the "White Cross Hospital." As a matter of fact, two German soldiers, after moving into the apartment where Iván lived with Erzsi on Abonyi Street, had given him these cans. Despite our hunger in the shelter, we could not open them because we did not have a can opener. We set the cans aside, promising one another to take them along when we went home one day and eat them for lunch in our apartment on Abonyi Street. In fact, I dreamed about it all the time: we were sitting around the table in our apartment eating sardines. But this dream did not materialize. In vain did we try to tell the Russians that we had been starving for months, that we were desperately hungry, that we were Jews trying to go home; it did not change anything. They took the sardines away from us, together with my watch, which they had discovered on my arm. Then they let us walk on.

But that was not easy. The streets were covered with dead bodies, and wrecked vehicles were lying everywhere. Along the roads, overturned horse carts and dead horses blocked the traffic. We kept on walking, though, moving among mountains of rubble, alongside burned-out buildings. The destruction was unimaginable and horrendous. On the streets, against the background of demolished houses, some people tried to hack a dead horse apart to take home its flesh. Leaving behind the Eastern Station, we were nearing home. Now we just needed to walk across Thököly Street and pass the pharmacy of the Funks. A few blocks down, there was Alpár Street, where once Faragó had lived. Next we turned left on Aréna Street and passed the Vatican house, turning right on Abonyi Street. Although somewhat damaged, the street appeared in better shape than the rest of the city streets we saw. A small figure appeared in the distance. I started to run; so did she.

"I waited for you so long," Erzsi said, sobbing. "But I knew you would come home today."

EPILOGUE

Iván Abonyi studied medicine after the war. He practiced radiology in Budapest until he retired in March 2010. He married Mária Farkas; the couple has a daughter, Krisztina, and two grandchildren, Bogi and Áron.

László Abonyi reclaimed his pharmacy and created a rapidly growing serum institute after the war. Both were expropriated by the Communist government that nationalized all private property in Hungary in 1948. His applications for permission to visit his daughter, Zsuzsi, who fled from Hungary with her husband in 1957, were repeatedly refused by the Hungarian government. In fact, he and his wife waited seven years for their passports before receiving them. These passports were valid for several months. The Abonyis arrived in the United States in 1964. After spending barely three weeks with their daughter, son-in-law, and grandchild, baby Kathleen, László Abonyi died of a heart attack in Dallas, Texas.

Margit Abonyi continued to live under the pressure of the enormous hardships that characterized Jewish life in Hungary before and after the war. She returned to Hungary in 1965, ten months after the death of her husband in Dallas. She lived in Budapest until her death in 1971.

Zsuzsanna (Zsuzsi) Abonyi married István Ozsváth in Hungary. She left the country illegally, after the defeat of the Hungarian Revolution by the Soviet army in 1957. The couple moved first to Germany, then in 1962 to the United States. They have two children, Kathleen and Peter, and two granddaughters: Elizabeth (who is named after Erzsi) and Eliana. Zsuzsi holds the Leah and Paul Lewis Chair of Holocaust Studies in the School of Arts and Humanities at the University of Texas at Dallas, and István is a professor of mathematics at the same institution.

Julia (Lulu) Abonyi-Fenyő was removed from her apartment and driven by two Hungarian gendarmes to the tobacco-drying sheds of Tornalja, where the Jews were concentrated. On the way, the gendarmes shot her husband for "moving too slowly." In the middle of June 1944, she was entrained and transported to Auschwitz. Surviving in the camp during the summer, she was transferred to Bergen-Belsen in the late fall of that year. She died, probably of typhus or malnutrition, in the late spring of 1945.

Dr. Pál Abonyi was drafted into the labor service and dispatched to the Russian front in October 1942. As a Jew, he was not involved in military action but rather in the maintenance of road work. He either froze or starved to death, died of the torture the servicemen were subjected to, or of disease—as did 43,000 out of 50,000 Hungarian Jewish labor servicemen drafted to the slave labor camps of the Ukraine. But it is also possible that at the end of the road, after liberation, devastated by hunger, he was shot by the Russians for breaking into a grocery store and stealing sugar. He had two children, Magda and Margit, and three grandchildren, Viktor, Ildiko, and Edit.

Erzsébet (Erzsi) Fajó was adopted by László and Margit Abonyi in 1946. She studied biology and became a laboratory technician, working in a serum institute in Budapest. She died in 1995.

György (Gyuri) Faragó, the world-renowned young pianist, saved the lives of several of his friends after the Germans occupied Hungary in March 1944. He became sick during the summer, but he still hid people in his apartment throughout the fall of that year. Taken to the hospital in late November, he died of cancer on December 3.

Ila (Nagy) Frank and **Sándor Frank** were taken from Kiskunfélegyháza to the brick plant at Kecskemét. Entrained to Auschwitz, they were killed, probably on arrival.

Erzsébet (Nagy) Kornél and **Dr. József Kornél** lived in Magyarkanizsa. Ghettoized in the pig farm of the salami plant at Szeged, they were taken to Baja and deported to Auschwitz, where they were killed, probably on arrival. They had one son, László, who survived the Holocaust and moved to Israel, where he married and had a child.

Anna (Anni) Nagy was sent first to the ghetto near the rail station at Szabadka. After being transferred to the entrainment center at Bácsalmás, she was deported to Auschwitz and killed.

Imre Nagy, from Szabadka, was transferred with his thirteen-year-old son, **György,** to the city's ghetto in early May. Like Anni, they were entrained in Bácsalmás and deported to Auschwitz. Both were murdered. His wife, **Cicus,** and daughter, **Éva,** who were identified as Christians by the Hungarian law, survived the Holocaust and moved to Israel.

Kitty and Robert Burg survived the Holocaust.

Márta Edinger (EDMA) became a graphic artist after the war; she was sought after and featured in the most prestigious Hungarian magazines and newspapers. Leaving the country in 1956, she settled in London with her family.

Hanna was shot into a mass grave together with 16,000 to 18,000 Jews near Kemenets-Podolsk in late August 1941.

Márta Karácsonyi and **Juti Bárány** were deported from the local tobacco factory, where the Jews were concentrated in Békéscsaba, to Auschwitz. They were murdered upon arrival. So were all of their former classmates at the Jewish Elementary School in Békéscsaba, except Thomas Altmann, who had escaped earlier to Norway, and Zsuzsi.